Cambridge Elements ≡

Elements in Public Policy
edited by
M. Ramesh
National University of Singapore (NUS)
Michael Howlett
Simon Fraser University, British Columbia
Xun WU
Hong Kong University of Science and Technology (Guangzhou)
Judith Clifton
University of Cantabria
Eduardo Araral
National University of Singapore (NUS)

SYMBOLIC POLICY

Laurie Boussaguet
European University Institute
Florence Faucher
Sciences Po, Paris

T0323920

CAMBRIDGE
UNIVERSITY PRESS

Shaftesbury Road, Cambridge CB2 8EA, United Kingdom

One Liberty Plaza, 20th Floor, New York, NY 10006, USA

477 Williamstown Road, Port Melbourne, VIC 3207, Australia

314–321, 3rd Floor, Plot 3, Splendor Forum, Jasola District Centre, New Delhi – 110025, India

103 Penang Road, #05–06/07, Visioncrest Commercial, Singapore 238467

Cambridge University Press is part of Cambridge University Press & Assessment, a department of the University of Cambridge.

We share the University's mission to contribute to society through the pursuit of education, learning and research at the highest international levels of excellence.

www.cambridge.org
Information on this title: www.cambridge.org/9781009478700

DOI: 10.1017/9781009290975

First published 2024

A catalogue record for this publication is available from the British Library

ISBN 978-1-009-47870-0 Hardback
ISBN 978-1-009-29095-1 Paperback
ISSN 2398-4058 (online)
ISSN 2514-3565 (print)

Cambridge University Press & Assessment has no responsibility for the persistence or accuracy of URLs for external or third-party internet websites referred to in this publication and does not guarantee that any content on such websites is, or will remain, accurate or appropriate.

Symbolic Policy

Elements in Public Policy

DOI: 10.1017/9781009290975
First published online: November 2024

Laurie Boussaguet
European University Institute

Florence Faucher
Sciences Po, Paris

Author for correspondence: Laurie Boussaguet, laurie.boussaguet@eui.eu

Abstract: Symbols are everywhere in politics. Yet, they tended to be overlooked in the study of public policy. This Element shows how they play an important role in the policy process, how they are used to shape citizens' representations thanks to their ability to combine meanings and to stimulate emotional reactions. It uses situation of emergency as a lens through which this symbolic dimension is analysed, and it focuses on two case studies (governmental responses to the Covid-19 crisis in Europe in 2020 and to terrorist attacks in France in 2015). The Element shows how the symbolic enables leaders to claim legitimacy for themselves and their decisions, and foster feelings of reassurance, solidarity and belonging. All politicians use the symbolic, whether consciously or otherwise, but what they choose to do varies and is affected by timing, the existence of national repertoires of symbolic actions and the *personas* of leaders.

Keywords: symbolic, policy, leadership, crisis management, legitimation

ISBNs: 9781009478700 (HB), 9781009290951 (PB), 9781009290975 (OC)
ISSNs: 2398-4058 (online), 2514-3565 (print)

Contents

1 What Is the Symbolic?

To say that the symbolic is an important dimension of politics is uncontroversial for many historians and anthropologists. They write about the ways in which power is staged in ceremonies and rituals, so as to appear self-evident, natural, or good whilst dissent is discouraged. They analyse how stories, images, objects, music, and gestures are strategically used to impress the public and to involve it in supporting order. For instance, Kantorowicz explains how conceptions of the King's 'two bodies' were used to smooth the transition after the death of a French monarch, the physical corpse of the deceased separating from the body politic of France, which would be passed on to his proclaimed successor (Kantorowicz, 2016). In a very different context but in a very similar way, Balandier writes about the staging of political power in traditional African kingdoms (Balandier, 2006). Ethnographic and historical accounts, photographs, and paintings depict the impressive spectacles of coronation ceremonies or of royal courts, where the powerful receive marks of honour and respect, and where sometimes decisions are taken. These representations (both as lived events or as depictions of them) present the actors in action and define their public, whether it is pictured or implicit, the audience being constituted by the readers, viewers, or listeners.

Let's imagine a scene, a council in which the main character is sitting (whilst the others are standing), wearing a peculiar cloak, speaking, surrounded by others. We would recognise her a leader taking a decision awaited by a public. The meaning of the scene can be deciphered by the audience. What the central character holds, and what and who surround her reveal where her authority emanates from; the crowd assembled represents the people upon whom she exercises power. Every detail carries meanings. All these are symbols, and symbols, anthropologists argue, are essential to human communication. Douglas goes further when she writes that 'it is impossible to have social relations without symbolic acts' (Douglas, 2002, 62). In this section, we define symbols and the symbolic and show how taking it into account sharpens how we can make sense of power, politics, and policy in contemporary societies.

1.1 What Are Symbols?

Symbols include a wide range of 'things' (Y) that a social actor or group of actors (A) uses to convey meanings (X) to another social actor or group of actors (B). This is possible because the meanings X that A and B ascribe to Y are co-constructed through agreements and disagreements (Wodak, 2009: 11). They are not an essential property of Y, but they are known by A and B and this knowledge is socially transmitted (through socialisation or education). By contrast, private symbols such as in dreams cannot be understood by others. Y is used in social interactions, and sometimes in everyday life as well, and there are moments when the use of Y evokes X for A and for B. This is particularly the case in social practices – ways of doing things that are socially transmitted and that structure social lives everywhere and every day. In these moments, recognising Y as a symbol is like an epiphany (Durand, 2003: 13) that marks connection with those who share such an understanding. Many other onlookers are oblivious to the messages that A and B understand thanks to Y. Symbols thus create boundaries in social time and space, boundaries that define communities of individuals – 'Not to know them is not to belong' (Hunter, 1974: 67) – who believe they share something, be it religion, cultural practices, abstract values or even the imagination of shared experiences (Anderson, 1991). However, symbols can also be missed, or misinterpreted: indeed, A may use Y to convey X to B, but B may for reasons of her own fail to read (or 'decode') it appropriately, whilst C, on the contrary, recognises it as a symbol but, unanticipated or hoped by A, she interprets it as Z.

The meanings X that A seeks to associate to Y belong to the realm of ideas and imagination: they are abstractions and concepts, some of which would be difficult to fully define (Godelier, 2015), such as state or nation. Because there is often more than one meaning attached to Y, its use in any given context is ambivalent and sometimes it is plural (polysemic). For instance, the colour red is, for obvious reason, often associated with blood. Henceforth, it has also come to be associated with life, strength, joy, power, force or, in a rather different vein (no pun intended!), with menstruation, wounds, impurity, violence, death, or revolution (amongst other things). Is the red robe worn by a character referring to her power, to joy or death or to her gender? Or does it evoke several of these meanings simultaneously? Thus, while symbols are convenient ways of communicating mental images, their meanings are often ambiguous, plural, and complex (Turner, 1970: 27). They require an interpretation, which is contextual and often influenced by the presence of other symbols (Deflem, 1991). These qualities make symbols creative resources for artists. Symbolism, in art or in politics, refers to the deliberate and systematic use of symbols with the intention of communicating a message.

Thus, symbols are 'evocative devices' (Turner, 1969: 42): they guide perceptions and understandings; they evoke ideas. As such, they are resources for power and power struggles, and are thus intrinsically political. They present a 'reality' that appears as self-evident, and behaviours that are appropriate to the circumstances. Furthermore, symbols articulate the realm of the imaginary (abstractions) with emotions connected with the socialisation into their meanings: they touch and move those who recognise them (Turner, 1970); they carry evaluative judgment and emotional attachments (Göhler, 2013: 104). They combine two dimensions that may greatly influence the audience: a cognitive content on the one hand (expression of ideas that cannot be easily spelt out) and a physical or embodied register on the other hand, that stimulates emotions (like empathy, fear, or anger) and entices the public to act or react (Turner, 1970). As a consequence, symbols are often seen as prescriptive and generally as restricting critical inquiry or the expression of dissent. Finally, symbols are rarely used on their own but combined, such as in rituals. This can facilitate the interpretation of the meanings they are carrying. Now that we understand better what symbols are and how they convey messages, notably messages about power and the social order, we turn to contexts more familiar to us – contemporary liberal representative political systems, and we refer to 'the symbolic' as symbols and their meanings taken together.

1.2 Thinking with the Symbolic

Many people may consider that the symbolic plays an important role in the politics of traditional societies but still dismiss it as irrelevant to understand today's world because they associate it with magic or with religion. There are several reasons for this. First, contemporary societies of the Global North think of themselves as rational and modern and reject what philosophers of the Enlightenment deemed superstitions and obscurantism. The world we live in may thus appear as 'disenchanted' and secular, material and knowable through analytic and scientific enquiry. For people suspicious of religious beliefs, which Marx famously described as the 'opium of the masses', the symbolic is seen as something used to manipulate people – to lure them into acting against their best interest. Second, democratic governments hold their power thanks to legal rational procedures and the freely expressed electoral choices of citizens. The dominant argument is that there is no need for coded messages to lull people into submission. Third, the idea that there are fundamental differences between 'our' societies and 'others' is constitutive of much social scientific enquiry, including anthropology. Fourth, social and political scientists often embrace an approach that considers social facts as objective, objectifiable, and quantifiable. In so doing, they have invariably focused on eliciting causality links between them. Symbols are not easy to integrate into such approaches: the meanings they convey are context dependent and, as the effects they produce are about how messages affect the ways in which audiences understand and respond to them, they are difficult to assess or demonstrate. As many social scientists are uncomfortable about analysing this aspect of policies and of politics (Kertzer, 1989: 7–8), they have ignored the symbolic.

Yet, following in the path of Berger and Luckman, social constructivists argue that the symbolic is an integral dimension of all social life: the world we wake up in everyday is meaningful because of the collective representations we acquire during our lives, through socialisation and through social interactions (Luckmann and Berger, 1991). A few political scientists consider that 'there can be no politics without symbols' (Kertzer, 1989: 181), and thus are particularly interested in political rituals (Lukes, 1975; Abélès, 1992; Faucher, 2025). Some have even turned their gaze to mainstream political institutions, like the British House of Lords (Crewe, 2005), political parties (Faucher-King, 2005) or the parliament (Rai, 2010), to consider them in such a way. Moreover, political theorists are now paying growing attention to the connections between political claims, performance, and the political imaginary (Saward, 2010; Disch, Sande, and Urbinati, 2020; Rai et al., 2021). They also bring to the fore the multiple understandings associated to central notions – like the one of 'representation' – and the challenges of translating them (Diehl, Hayat, and Sintomer, 2014). Thus, although they remain a minority, contemporary authors in the social and political sciences question the social categories that structure and guide our thinking, and the symbols associated to them. Indeed, 'how can we possibly think of ourselves in society except by using the classifications established by our institutions?' (Douglas, 1986: 99). What should be clear now is that the symbolic is always involved in politics because symbols are inherent to communication within a social group, and therefore contribute to map social reality and power relationships within it.

1.3 The Symbolic as a Tool of Communication

Research on frames (Benford and Snow, 2000) has shown how social movements, the media and political actors shape perceptions and understandings (Hay, 1996). Thus, although political cultures are often assumed to prevent or slow down change, the social categories with which we think are not fixed. Migrants were for instance 'guest workers' in post WW2 Europe, but they are now often seen as economic, political, or cultural threats: access to social rights is restricted to specific groups and asylums claimants are detained in camps or on boats while their files are examined. As a new frame becomes accepted and established, it contributes to creating the realities to which it applies, because people conform to them and therefore behave differently (Becker, 1997; Hacking, 2000). Symbols play a role in framing activities because they participate to the creation of concepts and the naturalisation of modes of thinking in discourse. As such, they contribute to shift perceptions and conceptions, such as the boundaries of social groups. For instance, the

New Labour governments of Tony Blair, in Great Britain, relentlessly promoted the notion of the citizen-consumer, which infused their policies and contributed to change how British citizens understood their role in the polity and how they related to policy (Faucher-King and Le Galès, 2010). This influence of symbols on perceptions can also be more implicit, through staging and performance (Wodak, 2009: 31). One can think for instance of the turning point created by German Chancellor Willy Brandt kneeling when paying homage to victims of WW2 in Poland in December 1970: the event was a routine ceremony but the performance, which appeared as an unplanned gesture, transformed German identity and collective memory as it challenged the narrative of a country victimised by Hitler. The apparent spontaneity and the absence of a speech were important in creating the social reality of an acceptance by the federal government of responsibility and collective guilt (Rauer, 2006). In this case, the categories with which Germans could think about their collective past shifted because the performance conveyed messages that were commented in the media and received by the public. National narratives associating modern France and technology facilitated transitions towards a 'greener' society (Bess, 2003; Malone et al., 2017) whilst a discourse of accountability and transparency, associated with public choice ideas contributed to the emergence of an 'audit culture' affecting social and political trust (Strathern, 2000; Hay, 2007). Although less obviously, numbers and statistics are also often used in contemporary politics to construct evaluative judgements, associated with benchmarks and goals, such as concentration of greenhouse gases in the atmosphere. CO_2 emissions graphs and the thresholds identified by scientists as climate tipping points 'make as real' trends that publics can understand as incoming and potentially apocalyptic climate change requiring urgent political action.

These examples show that public policies include a communicative dimension that involves mobilising social categories that shift or shape collective representations. It is a resource for institutions and collective actors as well as for politicians, whether they are addressing their audience as groups or as individuals. Let us unpack this further: the symbolic is a means to communicate with or within a social group, whose members can understand what is referred to. It makes parsimonious communication easier because ideas can be expressed simply and quickly. For instance, pictures of the White House prompt American audiences to think of the office, the officeholder, and the institution of the Presidency (Druckman and Jacobs, 2015). The symbolic contributes to modes of thinking about politics that are intuitive rather than deliberative, and as a consequence faster and possibly politically expedient, but uninformed (Stoker, Hay, and Barr, 2016).

Yet, the symbolic is not a straightforward tool for communication between a communicator and her audiences. Symbols convey implicit, elliptical, and ambiguous messages that are interpreted by those who receive them – and liable to be misinterpreted. Using a symbol inappropriately may have consequences: when a tourist wears an orange scarf on the street of Glasgow, her choice of clothing may be interpreted as an overt assertion of her religious (protestant) affiliation. A Celtic Football Club fan may take this as the provocation of a Ranger FC supporter, exciting her anger against the nemesis of her favourite team and forget in the forceful expression of her sporting passion that it may also signify personal taste, an homage to Buddha's enlightenment or a reference to the 2014 Ukrainian revolution. Because symbols are context dependent, the mistake may not happen if the situation is contextualised by our hypothetical Celtic fan: the Dalai Lama, or the Dutch football team, is visiting the city. The ambiguities of symbols can also be strategically used. Let's imagine a politician wearing or uttering something that is likely to be interpreted as an invitation to violence or hatred by a social group but is devoid of any such meaning for others. If criticised, the politician in question can claim ignorance of the norms, claim innocence, and argue that her behaviour has been misinterpreted.

We have seen in this section that symbols are ever present in contemporary politics even if they have been neglected or dismissed by social scientists; that they are important means of communication between an actor and her audience ; that, to be felicitous, such communication requires that both share an understanding of the implicit as well as of the explicit meanings conveyed; that the use of symbols triggers emotions and reactions at the individual or the collective level; that there are many opportunities for such communication to go wrong because the meanings of a given symbol need to be interpreted by the audience and there is an inherent interpretive ambiguity in a symbol – it can symbolise different things and be associated differently; that it is not quite enough for actor and audience to share the knowledge about the symbol and its meanings. A sickle and a hammer appearing together may invoke little more than manual work for many observers most of the time. But at other times, or to others, particularly if they form a cross or if they are associated with the colour red, it is a reference to the Soviet Union. Read as such, the symbol is likely to stir evaluations and emotions, which can be contradictory: nostalgia or pride, hopes in a communist future or oppression, equality, or the opposite of freedom, good or evil. If so, it can also trigger different reactions, such as a call to arms to defend the country or the ideals of international solidarity between working classes, on either side of the Cold War front and in countries that have been within the sphere of influence of the USSR. Finally, it is quite possible that the meanings associated to the symbols used by A are, most of the time, not deciphered by the majority of lay audiences or are only partially understood. They may require an explanation that is nowadays likely to be provided by commentators, journalists, etc.

In this Element, we talk about the symbolic more than symbols *per se* because we refer to the vast array of objects, words or phrases, images, gestures, etc. that are deployed (deliberately or more inadvertently) politically and we want to avoid a restrictive understanding, which would limit symbols to the most obvious ones, from flags to buildings. We contend that we need to include myths, narratives, cultural practices and so forth, which also carry meanings that are intentionally included by social actors and are usually adequately interpreted by their audience. For instance, Indian Prime Minister Modi carefully adapts his wardrobe to specific public occasions, always wearing a traditional Indian, sometimes regional, attire and carefully chosen colours; Macron invited Putin to Versailles and Trump to the Eiffel Tower. We also want to highlight the combinations of symbols, such as in rituals, and how it helps the audience interpret meanings.

We talk about symbolic policy because every policy has a symbolic dimension and because we emphasise how policy makers work to shape the perceptions of their audiences and frame the interpretations of their actions, using the symbolic to convey meanings that are both cognitive and emotional. Section 2 argues that the symbolic has been neglected in public policy analysis and makes the case for taking it seriously. Section 3 shows that it is embedded in the claims to legitimacy that are made by political authorities, whether they invoke their roles as representatives, the process of policy-making or the outcome of their actions. We then take 'crisis' as a magnifying glass to analyse how the symbolic plays a part in reassuring the population (Section 4) and nurturing feelings of belonging and solidarity (Section 5). While we use many examples from widely different contexts, we also use our own research on responses to terrorist attacks in Paris in 2015 and to the beginning of the pandemic in 2020 in four European countries (France, Italy, Germany and the United Kingdom). These two cases are a leitmotiv through the Element. The two following sections analyse what can affect symbolic work and policy: Section 6 addresses the question of time and timing whereas Section 7 makes the case for the existence of national repertoires of symbolic actions and the agency of leaders in the selection of symbolic policy instruments. In Section 8, we explore the ways in which the effects of the symbolic in policy can be assessed. Lastly, Section 9 summarises the argument of the Element and its contribution to the literature on public policy and our understanding of contemporary politics.

2 The Symbolic: An Overlooked Dimension of Policy

Three days after the terrorist attacks that struck Paris on 13 November 2015, the French President addressed the two houses of Parliament gathered in Versailles. He announced his intention to change the Constitution to allow the withdrawal of French citizenship from dual nationals convicted of terrorist offences. Such a measure was quickly criticised as 'symbolic'. As noted by the French Council of State in its December 2015 published position, removing citizenship would have 'limited practical relevance'. The public debate asked indeed how terrorists could be dissuaded from acting when even death does not stop them. Furthermore, from the Government's perspective, the measure changed little since, although not enshrined in the Constitution, the practice of the withdrawal of French citizenship was already legal. So, the policy, which was perceived as having few practical implications, was 'symbolic' in the common-sense understanding.

Nevertheless, as seen in Section 1, 'symbolic' also refers to the power of symbols, and the proposed reform, by catering to several distinct audiences, illustrates this perfectly: it was a concession to the Opposition designed to bolster wavering political unity in the face of the second major attack within a year; it was also a message addressed to the entire population, whose cohesion needed to be reinforced. Repeated surveys conducted during the year had shown high rates of approval for this hypothetical policy. Public support for the measure was interpreted at the Élysée as an indication that the population considered that individuals who attack the country do not deserve to be French – since they have *de facto* already excluded themselves from the national community: 'we are in a logic of deciding who is included in the Republic and who no longer belongs (. . .). The Republic itself defines the shape and the limits of our Nation' (interview May 2016).

Public policies impact more than just the material world: they are symbolic because they shape cognitions, values, emotions, and beliefs. This analytic shift is at the core of this Element. Indeed, despite the assertion that policymaking involves the manipulation of symbols (Laswell, 2011), and although the founding fathers of the discipline recognised the importance of rhetoric, and of what governments say alongside what they do (Dye, 1987; Laswell, 2011), 'the study of policy has, for the greater part of its history, been neglectful of this absolutely crucial aspect of public policy' (Parsons, 1995: 178). Besides, for a long time, most policy science textbooks did not address the topic or presented it in a reductionist way: symbolic policies are policies that fail to solve problems, they are acts of political manipulation (Goodin, 1980). This section provides a survey of the public policy literature and identifies two explanations for this paradox – a problematic focus on the question and a misconception of what the symbolic is – before presenting our choice to focus on extraordinary times to bring back the symbolic into the analysis of policy process.

2.1 A Problematic Focus

First, the focus of policy analysis contributed to a blurred vision. From its inception in the 1950s, it has been characterised by a positivist bias. Initially conceived as both a science *of* public action and a science *for* public action (Lerner and Laswell, 1951), it aimed to generate knowledge to guide decision-making, rationalise the actions of public authorities, and ultimately resolve concrete problems in the name of (social) progress. Such a posture explains why 'analysts have largely been preoccupied with policy rationality rather than policy talk and rhetoric or "words"' (Parsons, 1995: 178). Thus, while anthropologists scrutinised every facet of 'power on stage' (Balandier, 2006), policy analysts systematically overlooked the symbolic. Of course, over time, the analysis of the policy process has shifted from its initial posture as various approaches emerged to overcome its limitations, broadening the conception of public policy to encompass not only the tangible content (such as the text of a law, financial allocations, or the adoption of a specific instrument) but also the speeches accompanying decisions, underlying ideas and values, and even non-decisions (Bachrach and Baratz, 1963). Cognitive approaches, for instance, direct attention to ideas, beliefs, values, knowledge, and perceptions shaping policies (RFSP, 2000; Bevir and Rhodes, 2010; Surel, 2019), exemplified by Peter Hall's policy paradigm (Hall, 1993). They posit that a policy represents 'the place where a given society builds its relationship to the world' and 'a process through which a society elaborates representations to understand, address, and act on the real world, as it is perceived' (Muller, 2018: 51–52). However, these authors don't specifically consider the use of symbols and seldom account for the diverse publics targeted by policies – an issue that recognising the symbolic dimension of public policies arguably helps us to address, as the symbolic is a realm of communication that suggests different challenges of communicating with different audiences (Section 1).

Sometimes, the symbolic is taken into account, but without being explicitly named or recognised for what it is. Consequently, its specificity is missed. This is notably the case in the literature on what is called 'policy feedback', which demonstrates that public policies have an impact on citizens' political behaviours, that they lead to the construction of a constituency that may create its own interest groups and shape future public action. In short, it is argued that (some) policies do contribute to shaping their public – not only their social representations but also their actions – as Schattschneider had announced in 1935 – 'new policies create new politics' (Schattschneider, 1935: 288). More precisely, policies are said to have two kinds of effects on citizens: a 'resource' effect and an 'interpretative' one (Dupuy and van Ingelgom, 2019). In the first case, policies contain, propose, and decide how resources (money, time, rights, social benefits, etc.) are used and distributed, how they create incentives (and costs) that influence citizens' behaviours. The second effect is cognitive and refers to the capacity of a policy to modify individual and collective representations. Indeed, policies articulate ideas about the problem to solve, identify its cause and those responsible for the situation, and propose solutions, which are presented as the right thing to do. At each step, individuals' perceptions, beliefs, identities, representations, or feelings of belonging are susceptible to change. This is what Mettler showed with the case of the GI Bill in the USA (Mettler, 2005): the bill not only gave former soldiers the opportunity of a free education, but it also influenced their perceptions. Grateful for the great opportunity they had been granted, many felt liable to the community. This translated into higher levels of civic participation. One can consider that the policy served as a symbol, which was interpreted by GIs as a society's gift to them. This second kind of effect, interpretative, is clearly symbolic since it affects citizens' social representations (how they make sense of the world).

Yet, as the symbolic is neither named nor recognised in the literature on policy feedback, it is misunderstood. Indeed, this strand of the literature usually bypasses the intentions of policymakers. It overlooks how policies are presented and justified, the choice of images, lexicon, and narratives. Similarly, it does not consider the ambiguity of the messages that policies convey. We argue that to understand the role played by the symbolic in public policies, one should not be concerned solely with the resource or material effects they may have on, and for, citizens. Instead, one also needs to consider policies as a dialogue with citizens' representations or perceptions. Through policies, policymakers talk to individual and collective representations: they draw from them, they try and maintain, reinforce, or modify them. They do so because they mobilise the symbolic. It is important to name it as such because failing to do so deprives the analyst of the capacity to reflect on its specificities. Unnamed, it is invisible and impossible to disentangle it from the context. Acknowledging its presence in public policies means that it can be brought back into the analysis.

Finally, some scholars (like Rein, 1976; Roe, 1994; Yanow, 1996 and 2000) challenged positivist research methods in policy analysis by developing an interpretive approach (IPA) focusing on human subjectivity in a historical and cultural context. While it does not constitute a unified school, these works collectively assume that the policy process, to be properly understood, must be analysed through what it means for the actors involved (Bevir and Rhodes, 2003). In essence, 'an interpretive approach to policy analysis (...) is one that focuses on the meanings of policies, on the values, feelings, or beliefs they express, and on the processes by which those meanings are communicated to and 'read' by various audiences' (Yanow, 2000: 14). Interpretive approaches place the symbolic at the core of the analysis because they 'explore not only "what" specific policies mean but also "how" they mean' (Yanow, 2000: 8). To achieve this, they study the means and processes through which policy meanings are communicated to different audiences. Generally, these meanings are transmitted through artefacts, language, or acts.

We share some important premises with the IPA, such as the importance of considering a policy in a broad way, recognising the power of the symbolic, understanding its crucial dimension in policy process, and adopting a qualitative methodological approach. Yet, our focus in this Element is different. We introduce the idea that, some of the time at least, policy makers intentionally use the symbolic. Moreover, our goal is not to understand the meanings of a policy in different interpretive communities, but to analyse the use of the symbolic by one of these communities, that of the decision-makers. We argue that one should pay attention to their intentions when they have recourse to it, to the choices they make, and to the messages they aim to convey through them. Our research focus is the intentional inclusion of the symbolic in the policy process for communication with citizens' perceptions and representations; it is not the policy as a symbol interpreted by various groups of actors (decision-makers, stakeholders, administrative agents, and citizens).

The oversight of the symbolic in policy analysis can therefore be attributed to a problem of focus that persisted over the years. Initially, there was a positivist bias at the inception of the discipline, followed by a reluctance to consider the audiences of policy and to explicitly name the symbolic in order to grasp its specificity. Subsequently, there was an emphasis on the meanings of policy and its symbolic dimension, rather than a direct focus on the symbolic itself and its utilisation by decision-makers. Another factor contributing to the neglect of the symbolic in policy analysis is the often narrow conceptualisation of the symbolic, even among scholars who have delved specifically into symbolic policies.

2.2 Misconception and Myopia

The policy science literature commonly dichotomises the 'symbolic' and material reality. Concrete actions are seen as having quantifiable and tangible effects, while symbolic measures are deemed less substantive. Mazur, for example, posits that 'symbolic reform occurs when policies designed to address certain social problems fail to effectively solve those problems' (Mazur, 1995: 2). She categorises French policies on work equality adopted since 1958 on a spectrum ranging from 'highly symbolic' policies (those largely without substantive impact) to 'material' policies (Mazur, 1995). In this context, symbolic policies are perceived as lacking 'real' output since they incur no administrative or financial costs, do not influence the general allocation of resources, and do not give rise to 'constituencies' or networks of actors ready to mobilise in their support (Pierson, 1993). In essence, symbolic policies announce intentions but do not translate them into action. They reside in the realm of discourses and can be viewed as 'flagging policies' or 'policies of display' (Suarez, 2014).

Moreover, Edelman, usually regarded as the undisputed authority on symbolic politics, insists on the strategic political uses of words, metaphors, and images by political actors. He argues that, at times, the symbolic is viewed as the solution itself – announcing that something will be done, or has been done, may be just as crucial as actually addressing the problem. A compelling example can be seen in the British Government's declaration that Brexit was 'done' in February 2020, a statement reiterated by Johnson upon leaving office in July 2022. This idea is succinctly captured in the subtitle of Edelman's renowned book: 'Political Languages. Words that succeed and policies that fail' (Edelman, 1977). However, despite being widely cited and influencing many scholars (Yanow, 1996: 16), Edelman inadvertently contributed to constraining the analytical potential of the symbolic. To some extent, he framed politics as a 'spectacle' (Debord, 1967; Edelman, 1988), where political leaders use symbols to pacify citizens, maintain social order, and conceal inequalities and injustices. Edelman argues that policies are powerful tools shaping expectations, representations, and beliefs – 'government constantly shapes and reflects the myths by which the well-to-do and the aspirants to their roles live' (Edelman, 2013: 56). Yet, he posits that political symbols are intentionally wielded by leaders to manipulate public perceptions, obscuring the reality of social relations.[1] Paradoxically, although Edelman opposed academic perspectives grounded in assumptions of actors' instrumental rationality, he portrays political leaders as driven by self-interest and conspiring to influence the perceptions and beliefs of their followers.

These two approaches underscore a crucial and intriguing aspect of the symbolic dimension of political agency: its capacity to shape the perceptions and representations of members within a social group. However, both approaches adopt a negative, restrictive, and cynical perspective on the nature

---

[1] The literature on semiotics in public policies also argues that narratives, rhetoric and the symbolic are used for many ends, particularly hiding interests and promising goals that are unlikely to be met (Atkinson, 2019).

of the symbolic. In contrast, our argument is that words and actions are both important. We contend that the use of symbols does not inherently involve malevolent manipulation of the public, and that efficiency and symbolisation can complement each other. Indeed, there are public policies that not only address problems but also concurrently transform people's perceptions and representations. A noteworthy example of this accomplishment is evident in European welfare states after World War II: not only did they reduce mortality rates, but they also fostered values of social equality and solidarity within their populations (Permoser, 2012).

Lastly, the myopia hindering policy sciences from thoroughly considering the symbolic dimension is compounded by another limitation: the failure to recognise and engage with research fields, beyond the analysis of the policy process, that take the symbolic seriously. One notable example is the branch of research in democratic theory that endeavours to incorporate the symbolic and the imaginary into both theoretical and empirical analyses (Diehl, 2015) and advances the concept of symbolic representation. While the research topic differs, there are shared foundational principles with this approach. We believe, for instance, that studying the performativity of leaders and the many ways in which they use their bodies on stage is crucial as they unveil the political imaginary (the collectively shared representations of a specific role or institution) and can effectively convey messages to the audience – the citizens. Additionally, considering collective ideas and symbolic practices is vital for filling the research gap in policy analysis (rather than democratic theory) and establishing a foundation for investigating the symbolic dimension in policies. Consequently, we advocate for an enhanced dialogue with this body of literature, particularly to gain deeper insights into the role of the symbolic in the legitimisation processes of the political order and the policy process (see Section 3).

2.3 A Focus on Extraordinary Times

The symbolic dimension can be perceived as present in every policy, but we contend that it is most evident during times of crisis. A crisis, by definition, is a moment in which the established order is suspended, posing a threat to social stability, and challenging the legitimacy of those in authority. We take crises here as focusing events, in part because the upheaval necessitates decisive intervention and possibly more symbolic work than usual. Consequently, they provide us with an opportunity to showcase and better comprehend how symbols operate within policies (Hay, 1996).

In times of crises, there is a tendency for the population to turn to its leadership, whose performance becomes a focal point. While the leader is a symbol herself (of the nation, the state, the regime, and the collective in general), there are additional expectations regarding her ability to demonstrate authority, decisiveness, and to guide the collective effort toward resolving the emergency situation. The symbolic becomes particularly valuable because it allows for the communication of succinct messages that condense meanings and articulate various linguistic and imaginative registers that are instantly recognisable by the audience (Section 1). Firstly, the disruption of the taken-for-granted constricts the capacity to develop too explicit and long explanations and justifications, which are likely to be more contested and debated. Secondly, information tends to be scarce and unreliable in situations of emergency and, as social actors face a lack of information, they are likely to turn to authorities as authoritative sources. This situation offers political leaders an advantage in articulating an interpretative frame – with strong images, simple concepts, historical references, etc. – before other groups, including the Opposition, propose theirs. Although individuals and social groups may interpret critical moments differently, the public's perception of events can therefore be influenced – even if digital technologies have eroded this slight time advantage (Rosa, 2020).

In this section, we argued that, to a large extent, analysists of public policy have tended to overlook the symbolic. Such myopia has led scholars to miss important aspects of policy and policymaking, such as the efforts of policymakers to influence the perceptions and understandings of their audiences. In what follows, we analyse core tasks of crisis leadership, and more precisely the use of the symbolic to respond to crises. Drawing examples from our own research, we show how the symbolic shapes or attempts to shape collective representations, in order to legitimise the leaders in charge and their decisions, reassure the population and (re)create or maintain unity within the population.

3 The Symbolic and Legitimacy

All governments are confronted with the necessity of justifying their position and their decisions to those in whose name they govern. It is commonplace to say that the use of force is one of the characteristics of political power but, in practice, it is never sufficient to sustain it in the long term. Indeed, the legitimacy of governments is never better expressed than when the fist is in a velvet glove, that is when consent is granted without fear and without the use of force and based on both belief in the legitimacy of the political system and trust (Easton, 1975: 447). However, whether compliance is linked to habit, the absence of resistance or to support, it cannot be taken for granted: the order of things is constantly confronted with contingencies, and the legitimacy of governments is both subjective and fragile, susceptible to challenges as well as to doubts. Thus, governing elites must continuously assert the goodness of the social order, emphasising its role in providing the desired conditions of peace and prosperity. They also must secure legitimacy for themselves and their decisions, tirelessly working to demonstrate their trustworthiness and their capacity to maintain this order.

Our aim in this section is not to delve into political legitimacy per se, but rather to comprehend how political elites legitimise themselves and their decisions through the policy process. We argue that they do so in ways that are highly symbolic (deploying symbols), particularly in times of emergency, when citizens may have good reasons to believe that those in charge are neither in control, nor living up to expectations, and suspect that they are trying to mask their failures or their incompetence. Then, the political elites need to convincingly perform the role of an effective and responsible government, and this is particularly important for democratic governments, who also strive to demonstrate that they are transparent and accountable. They deploy many symbolic strategies to fulfil these ends.

3.1 Playing the Game

In line with works on representation in political theory (Diehl, Sintomer, and Hayat, 2014), we contend that a leader symbolically constructs both her legitimacy and that of her decisions, as she, in herself, is a symbol (e.g. King Charles III stands for the Crown, for the country, for the parliamentary monarchy). As the representative of the state, or of a democratic government, she may expect that her actions and words be thought more credible and notable because of her status. Embodying a political function, an institution, and the associated ideals, virtues, and values, the leader stands for something greater than herself when she speaks. In contemporary France, the President of the Republic is often referred to as the 'PR' by governmental teams. Interestingly, the acronym/ nickname phonetically resembles 'père' (father), and this linguistic connection is neither insignificant, nor surprising: the metaphor of nation as family and of government as parent is well known (Lakoff, 2002). Moreover, in times of crisis, leaders often take on the role of the 'father of the Nation', as President Hollande did in 2015, listening to French people and providing reassurance (Boussaguet and Faucher, 2018: 101).

This last example prompts consideration of the notion that merely assuming a role may not suffice; a leader must also execute and perform it effectively (Hay, 2009). Like theatre, where diverse registers (tragic, comic, dramatic, etc.) coexist to guide acting, everyday life (Goffman, 1990) and the political scene are governed by codes and rules influencing individuals' behaviours. As Diehl explains (2015: chapter 4), the performativity of the body (staging, gestures, images, etc.) is pivotal in representing an office. Thus, in each society there exist staging codes, that encompass verbal communication, body language, postures, clothing, facial expressions and even voices, and a leader must respect them and fulfil her role, incorporating body-performative elements, to be perceived as fully legitimate (Rai, 2015). For instance, a president must behave as one and abide by the unwritten codes aligned with audience expectations, along with the rituals and protocol defining the role, all of which carry high symbolic significance (Seligman et al., 2008). Interestingly, successful performances often go unnoticed and are perceived as 'normal' (Diehl, 2015: chapter 5), as seen in Angela Merkel's sober delivery of her pandemic speech in 2020. Conversely, violations of staging codes and the disregard for symbolic traditions associated with the role can lead to the discrediting of the political leader. When Alex Stubb was the Finnish Prime Minister for instance, critics 'panned his informality as not serious – objecting to, among other things, the fact that he occasionally wore shorts'.[2]

Arguing that a leader legitimises herself and her decisions by playing the game, respecting codes, and acting in accordance with the occupied function and chosen role involves recognising the presence of an audience. This acknowledgement underscores the interaction between the leader and the audience as foundational to legitimacy. This premise aligns with a growing body of literature in political theory that, over the past decades, has fruitfully discussed the concept of representation by drawing attention to the fact that it is best understood as a claim (Saward, 2010; Diehl, Sintomer, and Hayat, 2014; Rai et al., 2021). The argument is that political actors claim to an audience that they are representatives of (some or all of) the people, or that they are acting on behalf, or in the interest, of those they represent, and that they are authorised to do so and accountable for it. The performance of the claim constructs simultaneously the representative and the represented, and it does so by raising the saliency of some traits, or others, according to contexts. For instance, whom does an MP for Cardiff represent? Is it the people who voted for her, those who will vote for her next time, the residents, British citizens, those with a voice, or even those without, such as the too-young-to-vote or migrants? The MP can claim to represent each category at different times and to different audiences. It is the response of the audience that gives any efficacy to what she claims, and the audience varies (if she is thanking her voters, if she is doing her maiden speech in the House of Commons, if she is addressing the party conference, or if she is

---

[2] Duxbury, C. (2024). 'Alexander Stubb quit politics. Now he's favorite for Finnish president'. *Politico*, 23/01/2024, www.politico.eu/article/finland-alexander-stubb-quit-politics-now-favorite-for-finnish-president-elections-haavisto/.

invited on a radio show). The absence of denial can be interpreted as acceptance of the claim. It also can be seen as a recognition of the claim-maker's legitimacy.

Following this line of reasoning, we posit that, beyond the representative claim, which, if accepted, establishes the legitimacy of political leaders, they regularly engage in the performance of 'legitimacy claims'. These claims are integral to making their decisions acceptable and securing compliance from citizens. The strategies employed in articulating these claims leverage the 'imaginary' of the audience, drawing upon repertoires of narratives, myths, metaphors, and semantic and aesthetic information (Edelman, 1977: 34). In essence, they rely heavily on the symbolic. The following parts of this section examine various strategies pertaining to 'legitimacy claims'.

3.2 Legitimacy Claims Based on the Will of the People

As an extension of Scharpf's work on input legitimation (Scharpf, 1999), we initially explore legitimacy claims based on the *demos* (will of the people), where decisions are framed as legitimate because they are made on behalf of the people. Two distinct claims emerge in this context. The first, occurring upstream of the policy process, centres on the designation of leaders: the legitimacy of their decisions originates from their election by the citizens. In representative regimes, legitimacy is intricately tied to attentiveness to the *demos* – its participation and its consent. In this sense, elections transcend being mere competitions between candidates, and the counting of votes goes beyond a pragmatic and mathematical task of sorting results: its ritualisation is a means to make the selection of rulers 'special' (in contrast with everyday practices) (Faucher and Hay, 2015). Voters, candidates, and electoral officers assume roles and follow scripts, which are repeated alike at every election, in buildings that are temporarily 'consecrated' as polling stations. They perform their part in public and contribute to maintain the impression that something important is happening. Rituals create a subjunctive world, a 'world-as-if', in which everybody appears to agree with the definition of the situation produced by participants (Seligman et al., 2008). It is for instance expected that losers and their supporters will recognise the individual or party deemed to have garnered the most votes as the legitimate government.

The second claim materialises once leaders are elected: governments propose policies that seem aligned with public preferences. More and more often indeed, political parties present their programs as responses to voters' expectations. Once elected, they argue that they received a mandate to implement their manifesto promises or they seek to convince voters that their voices are heard. Deliberation is thus essential to representative government: parliamentary debates, as well as many meetings are convened, so that issues are publicly discussed (Kertzer, 1989: 42; Cohen, 1974: 53). This contributes to creating the impression that opposing views have been expressed, whether dissenting voices are heard or not. In fact, when parliamentary majorities are strong, or when rules allow (such as article 49.3 of the French constitution), debates may be seen as redundant by the majority, eager to speed up the adoption of legislation. Yet, deliberation is a means to confer legitimacy to the process through which policies are formulated and, if bypassed out of expediency, it can become a symbol of the majority's disregard for democracy. As electoral turnout declines, the claims to legitimacy that could be based on electoral support alone are undermined because parliamentary majorities produced by nonproportional electoral systems may derive from a smaller proportion of the electorate. Concerns for accusations of democratic deficits contribute to a flurry of innovations designed to rejuvenate institutions and practices, like citizens' conferences, participative budget, citizens' initiatives, ballots, and consultations or other events labelled as 'direct democracy' (Michels, 2011; Boussaguet, 2016; Mansbridge et al., 2022).

Another strategy employed for this type of legitimacy claim involves using extensive public opinion research to tailor political messages to the targeted audience. In Italy, for instance, Prime Minister Silvio Berlusconi was a trailblazer in changing the use of opinion polls. With him, polls 'began to be conducted, not only for a cognitive aim but also to be used as a tool of political communication' (Natale, 2004). In the case of the American presidency, audiences are primed with images of the President as strong and powerful; public speeches are carefully crafted to incorporate phrases and images likely to resonate with the audience; the media coverage that is guaranteed for presidential speeches raises the saliency of the issues he mentions. At the end, the overall impression is that the President's agenda is aligned with the electorate (Druckman and Jacobs, 2015). Similar practices were observed in our research on responses to the 2015 terrorist attacks in Paris (Boussaguet and Faucher, 2018). Opinion and communication advisers provided specific recommendations related to the adoption of figures of speech, images, and messages to better respond to perceived public sentiments and moods. For instance, in January 2015, the focus was on republican values and social resilience, proposing policies directed towards education for citizenship and social integration. In contrast, advisers considered a more martial attitude appropriate for November 2015, with the executive's tone reflecting this shift. The President delivered a pivotal speech to the Parliament in Versailles, engaging with the perceived *zeitgeist* of citizens wanting to be engaged in the defence of the country, calling for people to join the 'Reserve', and announcing military strikes in Syria.

3.3 Legitimacy Claims Based on Knowledge

The second type of legitimacy claim relies on leaders' ability to convince citizens that she knows better than others what problems need solutions, what solutions best serve the public interest, what actions are necessary to implement solutions. Firstly, those in power can assert their own exceptional qualities and intuition. 'I understood you', proclaimed General De Gaulle in Algiers, on 4 June 1958, to an audience of up to 300,000 people. Such a concise and ambiguous statement meant that everyone, whether Algerian Muslim, Pied-noir or French may feel personally hailed and recognised – De Gaulle then convinced many that he was the leader who understood the sentiments and desires of the people.

Secondly, leaders can also leverage the expertise of the best available professionals to inform decision-making and policymaking. In this case, the legitimacy claim is grounded in the knowledge of others, particularly those deemed the best in their respective fields. Historically, executives have often relied on the perceived objectivity of science, viewed as a truth untainted by ideological, personal, or partisan interests. Expertise is thus expected to be closer to an absolute truth and, consequently, in the public interest. The role of science as a regime of truth explains the appeal of technocratic solutions, such as the formation of a government of experts in Italy, led by Mario Monti, in the aftermath of the 2008 economic crisis, or the establishment of independent authorities during the era of new public management. Tony Blair claimed that facts-based social sciences would allow his government to provide the best policies and declared, 'It's not rocket science as to what people want or need' (Faucher-King, 2005: 184). More recently, the prominence given to independent scientific councils during the first year of the Covid-19 pandemic illustrates how expertise is mobilised as a source of legitimacy. Many governments formed new advisory boards or convened existing scientific councils, symbolically using science to legitimise their decisions amid great uncertainty. Political leaders frequently referred to these scientific committees in their speeches to justify adopted measures and delivered their speeches accompanied by experts. In the UK for instance, Johnson regularly appeared, in a carefully staged setting, alongside the Chief Medical Officer and his Chief Scientific Adviser, in an effort to add credibility and weight to his policies. In many countries, daily press conferences by epidemiologists and other experts and consultants, became a new ritual for people. By presenting statistics on cases, hospitalisations and deaths, decision-makers were seeking to alert audiences to the severity of the situation. The numbers became the symbols of the gravity of the pandemic. The dramatisation of this information aimed to warn, to inspire compliance with restrictive measures, such as lockdowns and later to demonstrate progress. In Germany, Chancellor Merkel, drawing from her scientific background with a doctorate in physics, acted as the 'explainer in chief'. She used her expertise to didactically explain to German citizens the impact of contamination on vulnerable people and the healthcare system, further legitimising her assertions.

3.4 Legitimacy Claims Based on Results

Lastly, in alignment with Scharpf's work on output legitimation (Scharpf, 1999), political leaders and governments can claim legitimacy through their ability to act, and sometimes also to deliver and to resolve problems. For example, after the terrorist attacks in Paris in January 2015, the army was sent to patrol the streets in front of buildings considered potential targets. Their presence could be read in several ways and the plurality of meanings was acknowledged by the chief of staff of the Interior minister: symbolically, it showed the might of the state and the swift reaction of the executive, and it was thus a means to reassure the population; it could also serve as a deterrent. It is the most visible part of the activation of *Vigipirate* since the terrorist attacks of 1995.

Because the results of policies are not always very visible (be it the decline of numbers of teenage pregnancies or of burglaries), it is important for politicians to provide tangible indicators and measures for their success. In electoral campaigns, this translates into pledges and commitments. Once in power, decision-makers produce targets and give account of their action in relation to such targets. Numbers and statistics are thus used to showcase action: the number of police forces on the ground, millions invested, doctors hired, missiles sent to allies, reductions in unemployment, and so forth. One precise number, serving as an indicator of a successful result, can become the symbol of a good and legitimate decision and, by extension, of a good and legitimate government. The rating of a country's sovereign debt serves as a noteworthy illustration of this kind of claim: many national leaders boast about having the highest score (AAA or the famous triple A) as a symbol of excellence and good management – or invoke it to justify unpopular reforms.

Lastly, political authorities engage in various rituals of verification and evaluation, which include audits, the use of formal, technical, and legal language, as well as the organisation of public inquiries (Edelman, 1977: 118; Power, 1999; Faucher-King and Le Galès, 2010). These practices provide them with a platform to demonstrate their good administration and the positive results of their actions. Legitimacy claims based on results are closely intertwined with rituals that aim to demonstrate efficacy and efficiency and that leaders often deploy to reassure the population, especially in times of crisis (see Section 4).

In this section, we have observed how public authorities endeavour to articulate effective claims about their legitimacy and demonstrate their trust-worthiness. They achieve this by playing the game, embodying their roles, and developing legitimacy claims based on the will of the people, knowledge, or results – all these are symbolic acts. Conversely, symbolic gaffes are powerful catalysts for undermining legitimacy and trust in authorities. Numerous instances revealing gaps between claims-making and actual practices can be found in the unusual period of Covid lockdowns, when authorities imposed drastic restrictions on the freedoms of their citizens. Whilst the Italian President Mattarella appeared on television in need of a haircut, like his fellow citizens, Prime Minister Johnson's Chief adviser was caught traveling for leisure, an incident that marked the decline of the rally-round-the-flag public opinion effects the British PM had enjoyed since the introduction of the lockdown. Several months later, revelations of repeated violations (and cover-ups) of rules of socialising on the very premises of Number 10 led to a public enquiry. These incidents exposed double standards at the helm and Johnson was accused of being unreliable, incompetent, dishonest, and unfit to lead. More crucial than the Prime Minister's demise, the contradictions undermined trust in his Cabinet and his party and sapped the legitimacy of British institutions. The symbolic is indeed a double-edged sword.

4 The Symbolic, Reassurance, and Trust in the Future

When the French government declared a state of emergency in response to the terrorist attacks of 13 November 2015, what made it a reality to most French citizens was the visibility of the presence of fully armed military personnel, standing at street corners, in public transports, and in areas deemed sensitive. Between 2015 and 2017, we interviewed officials and policy advisers at the top of the French government about the responses to terrorist attacks. According to the chief of staff at the Ministry of Interior (interview May 2015), the deployment of troops met two objectives: deterring further attacks as well as reassuring the public. Soldiers in arms were meant to convey the message that the government was taking the situation seriously and managing it with resolve and strength (Section 3). Thus, it directly addressed feelings of insecurity. The UK was attacked in 2017 but the British strategy involved very limited deployment of the military. Indeed, according to a former Home Office minister (interview September 2017), the best way to reassure the British public is to demonstrate a quick return to normality. The objectives of the two governments were identical, yet they chose different paths because the presence of armed personnel in the streets – a symbol of the might of the state – would be interpreted on one side of the Channel as a sign of the governmental preparedness and, on the other side, as a sign that the government is not in control.

In a situation of emergency, a key task for the leadership is to respond to the emotional and practical disruptions that have been created and to demonstrate that they are taking action to support the victims and protect the people affected. Indeed, leaders and their communication teams are usually aware of the need to demonstrate that they perform their role according to expectations. Senior civil servants as well as political advisors play a part in ensuring that such a message is adequately formulated. 'Regardless of his perceived credibility or his image at that moment, it is from the President that one expects reassurance', wrote a political advisor in a *Note,* sent to the French President on 8 January 2015. The following day, an internal email to the close presidential team read 'the President must stay on the frontline. He must show that he is in charge, he must reassure, and decide. (. . .) It is from him and from nobody else that healing and reassuring messages are expected' (Élysée internal email, dated 09 January 2015).

Although rhetoric is important and contributes to establish frames of inter-pretation, symbolic practices are also crucial to speak both to people's emotions and perceptions (Abélès, 1991). It is because they are formal, highly structured, repetitive, standardised, and 'wrapped in a web of symbolism' that rituals can channel emotions, guide cognition, and organise social groups (Kertzer, 1989: 9). 'Rituals of reassurance and purification' help authorities 'to be seen to be in overall control of the situation (. . .); to avoid massive, unforeseen and uncontrollable public reactions (. . .); to reassure the public that every conceiv-able effort is made to get at the root of the problem (. . .); to reinstate the rationality myth in the face of turbulence' ('t Hart, 1993: 43). In this section, we consider the symbolic practices and the rituals that are deployed to impress people with reassuring messages that reduce uncertainty, assert governmental control over the situation and present the state as powerful and effective.

4.1 Reducing Uncertainty

The first step towards reassurance for a population confronted with the shock of a breach in the taken-for-granted nature of everyday life involves understanding what is happening. Indeed, the crisis management literature identifies 'sense-making' and 'meaning-making' as two of the critical tasks of leadership. The distinction between the two largely relates to timing: the first involves dealing with the sense of surprise and the collapse of routine practices; the second focuses on explanations. 'Leaders are expected to reduce uncertainty and provide an authoritative account of what is going on, (. . .) and what needs to be done' (Boin et al., 2010: 13). With this in mind, public authorities propose narratives to describe the critical situation (Radaelli, 2019) and build 'causal stories' (Stone, 1989). They explain what is at stake, they identify the causes of the problem, and state what needs to be done. Before social media and internet, when a breach happened, the public had little independent information and relied primarily on representations provided by elites (Baum and Groeling, 2010: 449). In today's world, public authorities have largely lost the advantage they previously had and must work tirelessly to contribute to frame the discussion (Section 6). Three strategies are generally employed to reach this objective.

The first involves occupying the stage to acknowledge and identify the problem. A combination of informal and formal communication can be used to provide the opportunity to articulate a frame to the public and attempt to define the situation. In January 2015, the French Government's effective media strategy involved a division of labour. The President was mostly seen in action and delivered a few concise and solemn messages, widely covered in the media. Hollande delivered a short 'address to the Nation' from the Elysée Palace on 7 January after the *Charlie Hebdo* attack, then again on 9 January after the resolution of the hostage crisis in Vincennes. He used both interventions to label the killings as 'barbaric', to denounce the perpetrators as terrorists. He also mourned the victims and stated that they had been targeted because they were symbols of the French Republic and of its values. The Prime Minister toured the broadcast media. The Interior Minister supervised operations and provided press briefings, supported by the Justice Minister. Other examples can be found during the first wave of the Covid-19 pandemic: to catch up on his delayed reaction to the arrival of the virus in Europe and the UK, Boris Johnson occupied the scene. He gave two exceptional and formal speeches on 23 March and 10 May; regularly attended the daily press conferences; was filmed attending COBRA meetings; and multiplied posts on social media (on Facebook and Instagram for instance).

The second strategy involves using the symbolic to explicitly say as little as possible: indeed, information is scarce – and not always verified. Saying little, and implying more, facilitates oecumenical interpretations. Whilst it is tempting to focus on words, leaders and their teams do not neglect symbolic practices. Photographs and clips of politicians arriving and leaving meetings are particularly helpful here: they show decision-makers in action and their commitment to resolving the crisis. The very presence of dignitaries, and their body language, say more than any speech: they mark the importance of events, of places, of people. They signal cooperation (working lunches and dinners between European leaders), alliance (Merkel embracing Hollande or Kohl holding hands with Mitterrand). If official trips of heads of states are planned a long time in advance, impromptu visits to locations of accidents and catastrophes are indispensable symbolic acts of crisis management and receive, as such, wide media coverage (Boin, 't Hart, and Stern et al., 2010: 85). They provide opportunities for photographs and films that evoke a flurry of intense activities. Thus, when President Hollande rushed to the headquarters of *Charlie Hebdo* in January 2015, it underlined, according to his communication adviser, how 'the President had taken the measure of what had just happened', considering it an event of national significance and requiring immediate governmental attention (interview June 2015). Similarly, the international community's support to France was staged on and immortalised by cameras: the eagerness of some political leaders to be seen on the streets of Paris demonstrates how seriously they take such images. The diligence of Hollande contrasted with G.W. Bush's much criticised decision to fly over New Orleans after Hurricane Katrina rather than land. Failing to visit the victims and express emotion, even if he had been filmed assessing the damage from his helicopter, was interpreted as lack of care.

The third strategy consists in de-politicising the crisis by proposing a non-partisan framing of the situation (Hay, 2007). Accuracy is required both to facilitate the practical response and to inspire trust. This can be done, for instance, through judicial language, through figures and data that are usually seen as 'objective' and factual or through a scientific discourse, that can be presented as truthful (Boin, 't Hart, and Stern et al., 2010: 83). The Covid-19 pandemic lent itself to technical and scientific justifications, and, as we have seen (Section 3), most governments used health experts. Whilst the ontological security of everyday life was shattered, science was used to provide reassurance and focus attention on cures and solutions. While numbers can symbolise the gravity of the pandemic, they can also serve as symbols of improvement and recovery from the crisis. Besides, several political leaders made full use of a medical and scientific lexicon: Merkel explained contamination, Conte talked about truth as an 'antidote' and claimed that Italy's 'DNA' was that of 'a strong country that does not give up'. He referred to a 'shock therapy' for the Italian economy and presented transparency as 'the first vaccine' (Boussaguet, Faucher, and Freudlsperger, 2023). In short, every leader's decision, speech, or move is a meaningful act (Mariot, 2007) that is interpreted and thus partici-pates in framing the situation and its implications.

4.2 Asserting Control

Leaders also typically feel that they need to demonstrate to the public that they are in overall control of the situation. They do so in part through the perform-ance of being in charge. Goffman has shown how individual actors manage the impression they give in everyday interactions in order to try to convince others that they are competent, reliable, and in control of their role (Goffman, 1990). Press officers (as well as protocol, routines, and established procedures) help politicians maintain the dramatic realisation of their role (Scacco, 2011), ensuring that they perform it according to character (Wodak, 2009: 10). Control can indeed be represented symbolically.

It is expressed first by the resilience of the leaders in the face of hardship. During WW2, as London was being bombarded and children evacuated, King George VI and his wife remained in Buckingham Palace: their decision was hailed as a demonstration of resistance and solidarity with the capital's population and much praised. When President Zelenskyy refused the US's offer of evacuation at the beginning of the Russian invasion of Ukraine in 2022, he may have had in mind this famous example. Instead of fleeing, he began filming himself on his smartphone in the streets of Kyiv, wearing a military outfit. His stance emphasised that he was sharing the fate of the population at great personal risks, but it also galvanised the mobilisation of Ukrainians. These decisions are not just acts of bravery: they are performances of an ideal of leadership, exceptional in hard times. Indeed, the role of heads of states involves, on so many occasions, standing up silently (or without their words being heard from the public), attending ceremonies stoically, by fair or foul weather and hosting foreign dignitaries. In these moments, their bodies represent the body politic rather than their own. Communication advisers ensure that their leaders' dedication does not go unnoticed: President Hollande reputedly hardly slept during the hunt for the *Charlie Hebdo* assassins in January 2015 (interview June 2015); the Elysée published photographs of President Macron unusually unshaven, tired, and casually dressed in the early days of the Ukrainian crisis.

Secondly, leaders are to be seen 'in action', even when the nature of their work requires that decisions be taken behind closed doors. De Gaulle ironically commented that 'De Gaulle' would not be content with a merely 'symbolic' role ('*inaugurer les chrysantèmes*'[3]): as the President, his mission was decision-making. Photo opportunities are manufactured when they do not present themselves: meetings are held in 'situation rooms' (such as the '*Fumoir*' at the French Interior Ministry or the Cabinet Office Briefing Room A (COBRA) at 10 Downing Street); leaders are pictured in conversation with advisors, experts or with their peers. In 2020, European governments demonstrated their proactive management of the pandemic by convening emergency meetings (in person and later virtually) and summoning advisory councils (*conseils de défense* in France, *comitato operativo* in Italy). Leaders visited sites of field operations: Macron

---

[3] www.ina.fr/ina-eclaire-actu/video/i00012497/charles-de-gaulle-inaugurer-les-chrysanthemes.

inspected Mulhouse's temporary military hospital, Johnson visited NHS hospitals, Conte went to the Spallanzani Hospital in Bergamo, where the virus was first identified.

A third strategy involves staging the determination of the leaders as they perform their role by adopting a particular *persona* (Section 7). The setting, the costume, the tone, and the physicality contribute to give context and authenticity to the leaders' speeches and their choice of words (Finlayson, 2021). This is particularly so in face-to-face diplomacy where leaders also sometimes outrightly flout the ritual to assert themselves (Wong, 2021). However, as we will see below, beyond the performance of the hyper masculine leader often endorsed by Vladimir Putin (riding horses bare chested for instance), there are many other ways to incarnate leadership. During the first wave of the Covid-19 pandemic in 2020 for instance, Merkel adopted a calm composure in her 18 March speech; Conte chose to have an explicative tone (12 March); Macron defended a 'whatever it costs' posture (16 March); and Johnson publicly made his oath 'to do whatever it takes to so that we beat it together' (23 March). Unsurprisingly, the vocabulary that is used stresses the control and the action in the responses to the crisis: verbs like 'to want' or modal verbs like 'must' as well as expressions that show political voluntarism and the absence of hesitation are abundantly used; the first person ('I') is meant to demonstrate that those in power do indeed take a leadership role; verbs are often conjugated in the future to highlight the speaker's poise and their control over the situation.

4.3 Demonstrating Efficacy and Efficiency

Finally, governments endeavour to convince citizens about the capacity of the state to face a crisis and to do so efficiently. National leaders work 'to reinstate the belief in rational procedures of government (. . .), to reinstate the rationality myth in the face of turbulence' ('t Hart, 1993: 43). Thus, they bring to the fore the successes, the good management of the situation, and the capacities of the government and of all other institutions involved (police, army, health system, etc.) to restore order. They do so rhetorically as well as through practices. In the days that followed the 2015 terrorist attacks in Paris for instance, the President praised the efficient work of the police forces and repeated many times, in his different speeches, phrases such as 'we are able to' and 'we can', he spoke of a 'Nation that knows how to defend itself, that knows how to mobilise its forces and that, once again, will be able to defeat the terrorists'. The Covid-19 pandemic has required European national leaders to demonstrate the resilience of the public health sector and their support for it: they praised the resistance of national hospitals, the quality of the health system – like the National Health

Service (NHS) in Great Britain – and the excellence of the country's scientists who would soon develop a vaccine.

The discourse of efficiency generally also includes a 'language of "learning" to provide reassurance that "lessons" of the present crisis will be used to prevent similar events from recurring' ('t Hart, 1993: 43–44) or that lessons of previous crisis have been learnt and will help the management of the current crisis (Boin et al., 2010: 117–122). Convinced that the January 2015 attacks were the first in a series, the French Prime Minister asked the Department of Defence to prepare a strategic document detailing a wide range of possible responses adapted to different scenarios, including coordinated and massive terrorist attacks. By November, the government was thus prepared and able to propose that the President declare a 'state of emergency' granting the executive extraordinary powers. The objective was to avoid repeating what had been done in January (interview with the ex-Prime Minister Valls) (Section 6). The report was also shown to the press – and referred to in TV documentaries – to testify the preparedness of the executive. President Hollande illustrated that he was react-ive and proactive and that the French State would use its might when needed, by ordering military strikes in Syria and the temporary and exceptional closure of borders.

4.4 Performances and Roles in Reassurance Strategies

Symbolic practices, such as rituals, are important because they demonstrate that there is a process to deal with the contingency of a crisis and that someone is in charge. Indeed, the symbolic works discussed above are performed by actors 'in flesh and blood'. Several elements are important to emphasise about them and their use of rituals.

To reassure citizens, political leaders are helped in their mission by the rules and routines of their function. Most of the symbolic work that is deployed draws from established practices: the very fact of repeating what is 'usually done' brings a semblance of order and continuity. The roles of heads of state are thoroughly institutionalised and codified in protocols. Indeed, the symbolic apparatus that accompanies official performances is meant to draw attention to the role, rather than the individual actor, and to confer to it an aura of legitimacy (Section 3). The personality of the incumbent is expected to disappear under the robe and the role, the tone, and the text; yet successive Presidents interpret their part singularly. While Macron embraced with enthusiasm the symbolic of the Presidency as one of the essential resources of his role in 2017, Hollande had found it cumbersome when he took office in 2012, considering that it creates a distance between the rulers and the ruled. However, his government made great use of it in response to the 2015 terrorist attacks. Then, he played the leading part in ritual performances that emphasised bodily engagement rather than rhetoric: he was economical with words, but physically present.

Furthermore, although rituals are assumed to be invariant and draw some of their symbolic efficacy from this ability to connect past, present, and future (Bell,1997: 210–211), they offer opportunities to deal with contingency, to introduce change and to make it acceptable. There always exists a space for innovation and even improvisation. For Kertzer indeed, 'ritual is no less crucial to movement of political change than to champions of conservation' (Kertzer, 1996: 125). This is important in hard times but is also present in situations that are less dramatic but nevertheless open cracks and create opportunities for destabilisation. Coronations and inaugurations are thus designed to fit the circumstances, and the masters of ceremony can introduce nuances to the ritual. For instance, the coronation of Charles III was an occasion to demonstrate how the monarchy is adapting to modern Britain, just as Elizabeth II had done when she agreed for the event to be televised in 1953. Moreover, although vigils and official mourning ceremonies for people killed in the line of duty are relatively frequent and tend to follow a tight script, those organised for victims of terrorism require marking their unusual and inacceptable circumstances. This often leads to the creation of original rituals, as exemplified by the Republican March in France following the *Charlie Hebdo* attacks. Finally, authorities respond to comparable circumstances by performing rituals, the meanings of which can differ drastically. The choice of emotions stirred, and actions justified by these rituals can indeed vary significantly. For instance, the rhetoric of mourning speeches after 9/11 allowed President Bush to prompt his audience to think of a fight between good and evil (us vs them), whilst other politicians sought to appease, finding the words to acknowledge suffering and heal the community (Simko, 2015).

Moreover, national authorities do pay close attention to the symbolic message carried by the choice of the 'master of ceremony'. The pandemic provided several occasions to take such decisions and it is most manifest in parliamentary systems, where either the head of state or the head of government performed. The two represent different repertoires of meanings and the choice reveals how executives think about the implications of prompting audiences with distinct mental representations – if anything, it demonstrates how the symbolic is taken much more seriously by political elites than political science would have it. In constitutional monarchies (Britain, Belgium, Sweden) as well as in parliamentary republics (Germany or Italy), the head of state stands above the fray of partisan politicking and is mostly absent from everyday political life. Their interventions are rare (Christmas or New Year) and are addressed to the national community (or the Commonwealth in the case of the UK). In 2020, ceremonial presidents and monarchs spoke to their country, bringing solemnity and seriousness as well as being a reminder of the reassuring presence of the national community. In France or in the US, the head of state is also the head of the executive power: the overlap between the two is a source of confusion and potential abuse (Mueller, 1985). However, in 2015, the French executive decided to capitalise on the distinction: the President was staged as the decision-maker, supported by a small team of relevant ministers (the Interior Minister overseeing field operations, the Justice Minister the judicial enquiry, and the PM ensuring coordination).

Lastly, the transformation of the world of information and communication has given rise to new practices, some of them ritualised in that they were repetitive, meaningful, formal, and rulebound performances. For instance, during the first wave of the Covid-19 pandemic, daily health press conferences contributed to building the reassuring impression that someone was in charge, that science was guiding the search for containments and for cures, that the experience was shared, and solidarity consolidated. Traditional broadcast media were the vehicles of such new, and time-limited, rituals, but they were complemented by the increased recourse to social media, as means to connect with citizens at any time of the day (De Luca, 2020) and to reach out to younger audiences: Conte's Facebook Live videos, for example, became a fixture of Italians' Saturday night schedules; Johnson posted short clips during his quarantine, appearing increasingly dishevelled as his health deteriorated but assuring that he remained in charge.

In this section, we have shown how leaders engage in symbolic performances to reassure people about the ability of the state to lead society out of situations of emergency and chaos. To do so, they strive to reduce uncertainty and to convince their audience that they are in control; they claim that the policy they are developing is effective – a claim supported by an emphasis on the use of expertise. Their credibility rests on their performance of symbolic acts (which are often formal, rule-bound, repetitive, traditional) and on their competence in adapting them to context. As we shall see in Section 5, the performance of symbolic practices also allows individuals to bond with a collective (the Nation, the party, etc.).

5 The Symbolic, Unity, and Trust 'in Us'

On 24 June 1995, Nelson Mandela entered Johannesburg's Ellis Park Stadium to greet the players taking part in the Rugby World Cup Final. He walked on to the pitch, wearing the green and orange polo shirt of the South African Springboks team. With this one gesture – the black president wearing the jersey of the (then almost entirely) white rugby team – Mandela embodied a nation united at last, after years of Apartheid. While the example serves to illustrate the exception, there are many routinised occasions for public authorities to reaffirm the existence of a community. Such is the case with the American Presidents' 'weekly secular sermon', a routine form of communication delivered 'for an imagined congregation of the people and the press' (Scacco, 2011: 74), which serves to maintain a link between the President and the Nation. We have argued (Section 1) that the symbolic allows the expression of ideas, such as the Nation, that evoke a plurality of experiences, emotions, and forms of attachment. During international sporting competitions, flags and colours are means to express belonging and sometimes cues to express emotions. Yet, feeling that one belongs is even more important in hard times, when solidarity is a question of security if not survival. Yet, this is not an automatic effect, nor a psychological reflex. In this section, we show how 'rallying' the community involves the use of the symbolic to draw in-group boundaries and make present the idea of solidarity.

5.1 Rallying around the Flag

In the United States, 'specific, dramatic, and sharply focused international events' that directly threaten national security are expected to have a positive impact on the popularity of the executive. This 'rallying around the flag' effect was initially explained by a supposed 'patriotic reflex' (Mueller, 1985) and by the reluctance of the Opposition to be critical in a context of crisis (Brody, 1991). After 9/11 for instance, G.W. Bush used a boost in his popularity to introduce the Patriot Act, a set of restrictive measures that sharpened divisions between 'us' and 'them'. The rich literature that ensued showed that this phenomenon is neither automatic nor guaranteed (Baker and Oneal, 2001; Baum, 2002; Hetherington and Nelson, 2003; Williams, Koch, and Smith, 2013) but largely eschewed a discussion of the flag or the Presidency as symbols of the community (with the exception of Collins, 2004). Moreover, international comparisons led to the identification of structural and conjunctural factors enabling it, including the type of political system (parliamentary or presidential). The multiplication of terrorist attacks across the world after 9/11 has shown how rally-around-the-flag effects vary according to the repetition of the attacks, the nature of the targets (anonymous or symbolic), the magnitude of the attack (the number of victims), the political orientation of those in power and the electoral calendar (Bali, 2007; Chowanietz, 2016).

Yet, much of the 'rally around the flag' literature misses how governments play an active and crucial role in building what is seen and analysed as a rally phenomenon, based on public opinion support. In 2015, the French Government briefly benefitted from the expected opinion boost. Whilst in January the shock suspended temporarily criticism from the Opposition and the media, the effects were short lived. And faith in the collective capacity to resist, as well as in the government to coordinate efforts to do so, was eroded by the succession of attacks (November 2015, July 2016). So, the executive delivered speeches constructed to maintain, or re-create, the mental image of a community united in the face of threat and organised rituals to unite the population and generate solidarity (Boussaguet and Faucher, 2022; Tiberj, 2022). They worked to avoid anticipated intercommunity clashes and produce an image of a Nation historically constituted by diverse social and religious groups. The comparison across time shows how governments' responses use the symbolic to construct exclusive or inclusive visions of the Nation.

5.2 Rituals of Community

Whether local or national, communities exist in the imagination of their members (Anderson, 1991), which is experienced through the performance of symbolic acts. Independence days, anniversaries of revolutions and military victories mark the continuity of the community through time, and they make present mythical times and the solidarity that allegedly existed then. Countries (or political entities that cannot find such shared founding moments) make them up. For example, the 9 May celebrates the EU, while the Monarch's birthday, jubilees, and Christmas provide similar opportunities to celebrate the United Kingdom. In most cases, the rituals and speech acts in which political leaders invoke the unity of the national community are highly routinised. Moreover, every country has developed over time symbolic practices, embodying a national community paying homage to victims of specific incidents and mourning unjust deaths, or opportunities to invoke and solicit solidarity. At such times, the executive draws from past experiences and chooses the most appropriate ritual from an existing repertoire of actions (minutes of silence, flags at half-mast, the singing of national anthems, etc.) and actors (heads of state or representatives of the community). In the UK, for instance, as Queen Elizabeth became frailer, the royal family replaced her at remembrance ceremonies and hospital visits – the chrysanthemum ceremonies despised by De Gaulle.

This also applies to discourse as leaders generally use set phrases and expressions as well as the first-person plural ('we' and 'us') to remind the audience of the existence of a community and their belonging to that community – the 'choreographed dance of pronouns' that enables to define the 'speaker-audience relationship' (Gaffney, 2014: 7). In France, such presidential speeches are called 'statements to the Nation' and the head of state speaks 'in the name of the Nation'. Calls to unity can be very explicit when risk of internecine conflicts run high. In January 2015 for instance, the French government had evidence of growing resentment between social groups and feared that further radicalisation would lead to violence. Consequently, public authorities' communication emphasised 'unity' as 'the only weapon' against terrorism and using a clear lexicon to insist on that point ('fraternity, solidarity, gathering, common, let's gather, unity, together, etc.') (Boussaguet and Faucher, 2018). In the early days of the Covid-19 pandemic, European leaders appealed to civic responsibility and solidarity, asking citizens to 'care for others' and 'protect the most vulnerable': Merkel explained how to take care of cherished relatives, Italian President Mattarella praised Italians' sacrifices and civic-mindedness, and Queen Elizabeth II asked people to act in ways they would be proud of. When national leaders are also members of political parties, they need to appeal to cross-partisan unity and get the support of Opposition leaders. Thus, Conte insisted on 'a challenge that has no political colour, that must bring the whole nation together' and Johnson promised 'we will beat the coronavirus and we will beat it together'.

Yet not all such symbolic performances of unity are routine. Facing a new situation indeed, leaders and their advisors adapt to circumstances, including by being innovative or seizing opportunities. Hence, words are associated with gestures evocative of national unity. This is well illustrated by the French President, in the days following the attacks against *Charlie Hebdo*: not only did he call for unity; he also received political leaders at the Elysée Palace, one after the other. Upon leaving the Elysée after a private and solemn discussion with the President, the Presidents of the *Assemblée Nationale*, of the *Sénat*, and of the Association of French Mayors, the leaders of the parliamentary parties and representatives of faith communities all professed their commitment to a united front against terrorism in front of cameras. In other cases, jumping on the bandwagon of others or picking up from other's initiatives is the best available option. In 2020, leaders addressed their fellow citizens on television, one after the other in the space of a few weeks, including those for which such an action was unprecedented. Moreover, several acknowledged or even participated in the rituals of solidarity (Collins, 2004) invented and performed by citizens on their doorsteps and their balconies: every Thursday from April to June, Johnson stepped on the doorsteps of Number 10 Downing Street with his pregnant fiancée to clap for NHS staff, as British citizens in lockdown did.

Innovations may also come from a leader's entourage. The impressive 'Republican March' organised on January 11 in 2015 in Paris is a good example of such creativity. The March was the interesting outcome of a division of labour between political actors: left-wing parties had floated the idea of a demonstration (unsurprisingly as this is a well-established form of expression on the Left), but its organisation proved too complex with such short notice. Whilst the Elysée, the Interior and the Justice Departments were absorbed in field operations, the Prime Minister's Office had more flexibility and stepped in to make it possible. The team in Matignon worked with families and representatives of political parties to design an oecumenical congregation. Plans had to be changed when, for the first time in French history, the President asked citizens to march with him (9 January 2015): 'I call on all French women and men to rise up on Sunday, together, to carry the values of democracy, freedom, pluralism to which we are all attached' (Boussaguet and Faucher, 2017). The Elysée and Matignon orchestrated a complex cortege designed to embody the unity of the Nation behind the victims: three highly symbolic groups marched ahead of the procession – the bereaved families, representatives of political parties and of civil society, and the executive surrounded by the international community of allies. To ensure that the event would be as inclusive as possible, participants had been asked to come without banners or signs of any kind. Slogans and songs were banned too.

The March turned out to be an incredibly popular and international media event: it was the largest demonstration in Paris since 1944 (more than 4 million people in the whole country participated); it was coupled with an international summit (more than 40 heads of state or government walked 100 yards arm-in-arm) guaranteeing worldwide coverage and attention. The silence of the crowd contributed to the eerie atmosphere and was only occasionally interrupted by the singing of the national anthem (*La Marseillaise*) and (highly unusual) ovations to the police forces and their protective role. The success of the event relied on careful selection of locations, chosen for practical reasons (accessibility and movement) as well as for their symbolic meanings – between the *place de la Nation* and the *place de la République*. All these factors contributed to give an impression of a united social body, which was amplified by the Prime Minister's speech to the National Assembly two days later. Manuel Valls coined the phrase 'the spirit of January 11', an expression which dominated the public debate for several months. Criticisms and a polemic emerged a little later (Baudot, 2015; Todd and Laforgue, 2015). Yet, what was important at the time was the illusion of adhesion, unity, solidarity, and consensus that was created and persisted for a few weeks (Boussaguet and Faucher, 2017).

The impact of the symbolic policy deployed in January greatly impressed the French executive, and it sought to reproduce it in November. It was of course impossible to convene a public gathering after the massacre in the Bataclan and in the streets of Paris: the state of emergency prohibited all public gatherings. Consequently, the executive had to imagine alternative rituals of community.

Thus, while organising a civil ceremony to pay homage to the victims on November 27 at *Les Invalides* (a closed and secured place), it called upon the population to partake in this collective communion. The President invited 'every French person [who] would like to participate [to adorn] the front of their residence with French colours, a blue, white, red flag'. Whilst Collins (2004) analysed the deployment of flags after 9/11 as rituals of solidarity and points to social pressures in local communities, the French example is initiated at the top: the *Service d'Information du Gouvernement* posted downloadable tricolour flags on the official websites of the Republic. The tongue-in-cheek appropriation of the presidential call to rally around the flag meant that some windows were adorned with three coloured undergarments.

Finally, rituals of community are sometimes a mix between established routine and symbolic innovation. This is, for instance, the case for the convening of the Congress (the combined meeting of both Chambers of the Parliament) in Versailles on 16 November 2015. The Constitution limits its convening to three specific circumstances – the accession of a new country to the European Union; the revision of the Constitution; or a declaration of the President of the Republic before the people's representatives. Thus, when Hollande decided to convene the Congress after the 13 November terrorist attacks, he resorted to an existing institutional arrangement. Yet, he used the procedure to stage the national and the political unity of the country after an attack that threatened and weakened the social order. Moreover, he delivered a belligerent speech, in which the word 'war' was used many times in the first minutes, and he announced a surprise proposal for a reform of the Constitution. It would make it easier to declare the state of emergency in the face of grave threats, thus reinforcing the government's ability to act against terrorism. When he finished his speech, the Congress members (deputies and senators) stood up to applaud and sing the national anthem (*La Marseillaise*). The image given was that of the national representation in unison, politically united behind its government.

5.3 Rallying Which Community?

If calls to solidarity and unity are common to all countries that face an emergency, it is interesting to note that the national community is generally targeted in these calls (Wodak, 2021). In 2015, the French executive called for a political and a national unity and focused its attention on facilitating a rally-around-the-flag. It sought to activate feelings of national identity, pride, and solidarity. The attacks were first framed as targeting France, the State, and the Republic (Boussaguet and Faucher, 2017). Moreover, European identity and solidarity always remain secondary compared to the national ones in citizens' imagination and French citizens are generally little interested in demonstration of Europeanness – indeed the presence of the international community on 11 January was belittled by the attention given to the crowds in the press coverage of the following day. Consequently, we cannot be overly surprised that the national community was the focus of attention and that references to international solidarity remained marginal in the array of symbolic policies that were developed in response to the attacks.

The same finding holds for the Covid-19 pandemic in 2020. Whereas the crisis affected European countries almost at the same time, the national community was the main focus of symbolic policies deployed by most governments (Wodak, 2021). Leaders talked to their Nations and invoked national pride in their speeches. 'The whole world is watching us, (. . .) admiring us, taking us as an example', declared Conte (11 March). If leaders turn to the national community, it is in part because their peoples do the same: for example, Italians sang the national anthem (*Inno di Mameli*) from their windows and on their balconies in the midst of confinement. Whilst there were few calls to European solidarity in some European leaders' speeches – President Macron explained that 'this virus has no passport. It makes us join forces, coordinate our responses, cooperate' (12 March 2020) – the discursive reliance on the Nation can be explained by the long existence of an 'imagined community' at the national level (Anderson, 1991), making it obvious and easy to rely on collective solidarity. The members of a nation, even small, cannot know each other personally, but they share experiences that breed feelings of belonging and their communion exist in their minds. References to the national community are thus available, well known, and their use is routinised. They belong to national 'repertoires' (Section 7) from which the leaders can pull ideas and symbolic tools to respond to a crisis.

Yet, in January 2015, representatives of the EU and of its member states marched alongside the French President, showing both solidarity and anticipation of further attacks across the Continent. Indeed, Denmark and Belgium were next targeted, in February and March. A few months later, President Hollande invoked Article 42–7 of the EU Treaty (a clause of solidarity amongst the European member states) in front of the Congress in November 2015: 'the enemy is not only the enemy of France, it also is the enemy of Europe'. Yet, credible calls to international solidarity are rare and far between, even when countries are tied by treaties and profess close relationships and even when they are affected simultaneously. Whilst the European Union or the Commonwealth could represent such communities of solidarity, these supranational entities are afterthoughts, as shown in the efforts to rally European solidarity against the pandemic in Spring 2020.

This section has analysed how the symbolic is used to foster feelings of solidarity and of belonging, to create or activate imaginations of communities.

Direct involvement in a symbolic event such as the Republican March of 2015, the funeral of Queen Elizabeth, post electoral rallies, or popular festivals in revolutionary France (Ozouf, 2015: 313–315), allows participants to experience such emotions in vivo. Indeed, the experience combines multiple sensory channels (Leach, 1976: 41), involving sounds and smells, touch, vision, and sometimes taste, allowing the reception of complex messages, which condense distinct meanings (Walzer, 1967). Such complexity contributes to an uncanny effect, which makes their use and their analysis challenging.

6 The Symbolic and Time

In this section, we consider how time, sequence, and timing affect the symbolic work of politics. Although linear conceptions of time dominate in contemporary western contexts since the nineteenth century (Jarvis, 2022: 27), the political time of representative institutions is often characterised in terms of cyclicality (as in the idea of an electoral 'cycle'). These conceptions influence the symbolic repertoires (Section 7) that are available to public authorities and the way they are used. Indeed, the management of such temporal tensions in everyday politics combines routines and path dependency with the performance of rituals. However, when contingency reasserts itself, governments find out that there is no simple, unique recipe that can be followed every time and throughout. Circumstances require that following of emergency protocols be complemented by a capacity to innovate and to adapt symbolic work at every stage. And this is especially true when the crisis repeats itself or lasts over time. Thus, we illustrate how messages are tailored to circumstances by comparing the French executive's responses to successive terrorist attacks in 2015 and 2016. We argue that the repetition of attacks made it even more necessary for the Government to show that, after learning from the past, it reacted better than before. We also analyse the specific effects of electoral cycles on the strategic use of symbolic repertoires.

6.1 Notions of Time and Symbolic Implications in Everyday Politics

There are two ways to consider the articulation of time and timing with the symbolic work of public authorities. The first focuses on contrasting conceptions of time and how they define distinct symbolic works. The second analyses the ways in which time and timing impinge on decision-making and therefore influence the choices of symbols adapted to specific contexts. In contemporary liberal democratic societies, there are two contradictory yet overlapping and coexisting views of time: one linear and one circular. Let's take them in turn.

Modern time is primarily considered as directional and consistent with scientific knowledge and history. It takes for granted notions of past, present, and future that are also found in much of the biblical tradition. Public policies were at first conceived within such a framework: the identification of a political problem leads to the development of public policy responses (Jones, 1970: 12 and 230–231). The great ideologies that dominate politics are built on opposite valuations of such a take on time. On the one hand, conservatives find legitimacy in traditional practices: preserving the past is a fight against entropy and decline of an idealised community and culture. We find these views in cultural movements: neogothic and neoclassical architecture is an expression of such sentiments that provide useful symbols of the glorious past; the Pre-Raphaelites are another illustration of a resistance to capitalism and the industrial transformation of England. On the other hand, progressives and liberals see progress as the promise of a teleological transformation of species and of human societies. Post-1945, imagining the 'future of the world' (Andersson, 2018) has been driving a never-ending quest for a better world and to make such futures possible. An array of symbols associated with both traditions is based on linear time: rituals that make the past present or prefigure the future through artefacts, performances (inaugurations, national and independence festivals), the use of grand old historical buildings (from Westminster to Versailles) or modernist ones (such as the Bundestag or Beaubourg) (Boussaguet, Faucher, and Freudlsperger, 2023).

Cyclical time is often associated with traditional belief systems. However, it also constitutes the base for the legitimacy of representative regimes as elections – and the possibility of political alternance – rejuvenate power by renewing power holders and making credible claims that democracy is about the will of the people. Elections are rarely analysed as rituals, yet they do much more than aggregate preferences: through the symbols they use – which differ from one country or political system to the next – they articulate distinct conceptions of citizenship, sovereignty, and good representation (Faucher and Hay, 2015). Moreover, as symbolic practices, they integrate participants within institutions and contribute to sustaining participation and democratic engagement (Coleman, 2013; Sczepanski, 2023) and their projection in electoral promises of a better future. They sometimes represent a normal and routinised way to change the symbols available to the political authorities. The 2022 electoral victory of the neo-fascist party *Fratelli d'Italia* may for instance constitute a turning point in the use of some national symbols which had been largely abandoned after WW2 (Section 7).

Let us now consider the ways in which time and timing impinge on policy-making. A favourite phrase of post-revolutionary France was that 'to govern is to anticipate': it drew attention to the legacy of the monarchy and to the promises and challenges of the new political regimes. It focused attention on linear or cumulative time and the need to plan for change. In this context, the legitimacy of public policy comes from the mastery of time and the promethean task of shaping the future. Moreover, to anticipate involves drawing lessons from the past to prepare in the present the solutions for forthcoming problems. Hence, public policy in ordinary times develops protocols and procedures to guide and bound decision-makers. Much of democratic governance involves giving accounts as a means to evaluate and retroactively legitimate policy-making in order to justify the potential of a renewed mandate. In case of failure, to avoid blame (Weaver, 1986), incumbents can claim that they followed due process, argue that they prepared for contingency or that their ability to reform was restricted by decisions and commitments made by their predecessors. In this vein, policymaking involves following a clearly marked path heading to an agreed destination. Such justifications are weaved in narratives, encapsulated in evocative signs.

The predictability of electoral cycles weighs on public policy, not only because it stimulates the production of electoral manifestos as collections of policy commitments, but also because it gives a strategic advantage to incumbents who can plan the rolling out of policies to bolster their support and facilitate their re-election. Symbolic policy decisions are thus also coordinated with career plans and political ambitions: it is one of the parameters taken into account by politicians and their advisors as they try and combine a symbolic language that articulates the institutional roles they embody, the *persona* they want to be identified with, the trajectory and biography they are trying to construct, and to participate in a grand national narrative that will allow them to reach, or remain in, power, but also to leave a trace in history. For instance, the young Chilean President, Gabriel Boric, elected in December 2021 represents a coalition of left-wing parties. He manifests his rejection of the elites that have ruled the country through his dressing style. For instance, he never wears a tie and considers that this choice demarcates him from his conservative and neoliberal opponents. It is also the electoral cycle that fuels the blame games of contemporary politics and the strategic decisions of incumbents and oppositions to attribute blame for policy failure, to take responsibility for decisions, or to try and diffuse attention or deny the very existence of a policy problem (Boin, 't Hart, and McConnell, 2009). Such jousting is a framing competition in which opponents attempt to impose their own interpretation of events, thereby legitimising the solutions that they advocate.

Regardless of whether time is unidirectional or circular, public policy is not only about building from experience to construct a future, but also about responding to contingency and making the most of it to present a rationale for it. Consequently, time is 'both a producer and a product of political intervention.

It is constitutive of political identities, processes, and actions' (Jarvis, 2022: 27). It is thus used creatively by political leaders. President Macron's interest in drawing from the symbolic repertoire of French history has been widely commented, including his alleged desire to be '*maître des horloges*' – to control time by bringing history into the present[4] but also by controlling the political agenda. His ambition has been challenged by a succession of unpredicted events: the rebellion of the 'Gilets jaunes', the Covid pandemic, and the wars in Ukraine and in Palestine. In the next section, we focus on situations of crisis to illustrate how specific notions of time are constitutive of the social construction of crises, the importance actors give to context and time in tailoring their messages, and their use of the symbolic in the process.

6.2 Symbolic Policy in the Time of Emergency

The literature on crisis is vast, and not our focus here. It has highlighted how crisis is constructed through the production of narratives of time, involving ideas about temporal discontinuity, logics of directional change or circularity that draw from the national imaginaries of selective memories about the past and projections into the future. Crisis management, thus, involves symbolic work at every stage, including the definition of the crisis itself (Hay, 1996; Boin, 't Hart, and McConnell, 2009).

Focusing events (to use a more neutral term) provide opportunities to observe symbolic policy decisions taken under stressed conditions – this is a situation of 'time compression' (Boin et al., 2010: 3) – in which, by definition, normal processes are suspended, and little can be taken for granted. Established procedures and precedents may be available and provide templates for responses, but they may not be fully adapted. Furthermore, there is relatively little time to consider alternatives as circumstances evolve rapidly and the responses of other actors are difficult to fully anticipate. During such periods, different chronotypes (Bender and Wellbery, 1991) can be used in conjunction. The analysis of official British discourses at different stages of the pandemic illustrates how the significance of the situation is initially played down ('difficult times') before being represented as 'the worst of times' in a lifetime or since the war for the UK and globally (Jarvis, 2022: 31). Shifting constructions of exceptionality provide justification for political decisions and their reversal, for the speed of action, and for setting a 'new normal'.

Considering such constructions of time allows us to reassess the fluidity of context and how governments contribute to create a liminal moment in which a decisive intervention can shape future outcomes. It connects with the processual

---

[4] Jeanneney, cited in « Centenaire du 11 Novembre », Virginie Malingre, *Le Monde*, 04 November 2018.

analysis advocated by Victor Turner, who studied 'social dramas' (Turner, 1995). He argued that all social groups follow similar processes when confronted with a breach of what they take for granted. Such situations (whatever their causes) lead to moments of intense turmoil until a resolution is found. Four (analytic) stages can be heuristically distinguished: the rupture that destroys the everyday normality; followed by a liminal period of chaos and upheaval where the social group scrambles to understand the situation; which leads to the articulation of reparatory responses, both practical and symbolic; and the final emergence of a new normal.

In the early moments of fluid contexts, the compression of time suspends the established modes of interactions and political debates. With an eye on how public opinion will judge their actions, and temporarily deprived of alternative sources of reliable information, both the media and the Opposition turn to the Executive, which benefits from an unusual advantage. Collaborators of the French President comment that such a time lag has shrunk from a couple of weeks to a few hours: thus, even if the Executive has the initial hand in articulating a 'narrative of what happened', it has become indispensable to 'feed the beast' according to the Chiefs of staff of the Prime Minister (PM) and the President (PR) in 2015 (interviews June 2015). Therefore, the Executive provides a drip of news items: photos and footages, interviews, and soundbites, or press releases to show decision-makers absorbed in operations (President's Press Officer, June 2015). In January 2015, the President arrived within an hour near the *Charlie Hebdo* offices, where he talked briefly to journalists. Cautious reactions were communicated to the press, formally or not, by opinion leaders throughout the day.

Over time, it becomes more difficult to control the inevitable and growing cacophony of interpretations (Baum and Groeling, 2010). As the hunt for the assassins started, news channels chased police investigators – making great use of the competition between rival forces to leak information (as well as false information) – sometimes arriving on location before them and having a phone conversation with the hostage taker before informing the police. They were so effective that the Prime Minister's Office acknowledged following developments both through the live feed of news channels and phone contacts with the forces on the ground (interview June 2015).

In the aftermath of the January attacks, several events were planned to acknowledge the shock, coordinate a collective response, and heal the nation. Collaborators explain how some of these were drawn from precedent: minutes of silence are routinely organised in French (and European) schools since 2001; flags are traditionally lowered as marks of respect; schedules are reshuffled and used to signal the importance of something or someone. Some of these (including the minute of silence in all public services) were announced on the evening of the first attack for the following day. The intention was to demonstrate – in the flesh and the lived experience of the participants – the existence of a community of mourning (Ledoux, 2022) and to show how quickly the executive was responding. The next day, the media broadcast and commented on the short ceremonies, allowing those who could not attend in person to vicariously experience the ritual. Yet, timing is important: in the rush to set up the minute of silence, the government created confusion in schools which had no time to prepare. Moreover, further shootings and a hostage situation complicated the operational management. The media widely reported on the few isolated incidents, exposing them as cracks in the serenity of the moment, to the point that communication advisors mentioned them as the only serious mistake they could see in their management of the crisis. It is possible that because the state routinely organises homage ceremonies for personnel killed in the line of duty, it overlooked the complexity of such an event in schools. If these symbolic responses were largely routine, the 11 January march was not. Despite the emergency and the pressure of time, it is indeed sometimes necessary to innovate or to adapt existing symbolic tools to respond appropriately to an ongoing crisis (Section 5).

6.3 Symbolic Policies, Long-Term, and Cyclical Time

Finally, it is useful to consider how repetition – how an isolated event becomes part of a series – bears on the symbolic choices made by governments in emergency situations. Indeed, Oscar Wilde warned us that 'to lose one parent (. . .) may be regarded as a misfortune; to lose both looks like carelessness'.[5] There are many occasions on which incumbents have an interest in presenting a policy failure – or a focusing event that may be interpreted as one – as an isolated incident. Yet, in 2015, the Government did the opposite and warned that there would be replications. It argued that it was unlikely that all ISIS-related attacks could be folded. Taking such a public position despite the criticism of the Opposition (particularly of the far-right) was a means to deflect future attribution of blame in case of repetition and a spur for further preparations. In anticipation, the Government requested a National Defence report on how to respond to a future major incident. When disaster struck, it was presented to the media to demonstrate preparedness (Section 4).

Interestingly, the plan included symbolic actions that would show that the government was doing more and better. Several suggestions were indeed implemented in November, such as declaring a state of emergency, stepped-up military

---

[5] *The Importance of Being Earnest*, Act 1.

action, and the convening of the Congress in Versailles. The latter demonstrates reflections on the textbook closure of the January social drama with a speech by the PM in front of the National Assembly (simultaneously with the Interior Minister addressing the Senate), a rhetorical *tour de force* coining an expression that endured ('*l'esprit du 11 janvier*'), which was met with a standing ovation. However, the PM's role during the preceding week had been discrete, reflecting the constitutional order. His speech was interesting because it brought closure to the political sequence of events – even though it only marked the beginning of the learning and accountability tasks. Following Turner's analytic framework, we can identify distinct phases: the breach (with attacks on symbolic targets on three consecutive days); the chaos (whilst the assassins were hunted); the reparation (the Republican March, the international meeting of Interior ministers, the homage to the victims, and the ceremony at the Prefecture in memory of the police forces killed); and finally the political resolution presented in a carefully worded speech framing the March as a moment of communion and as the demonstration of the nation's high spirit.

In January, the President had been seen but not heard. In November, as set out in the plan, Hollande promptly gathered the two houses of Parliament for a rallying speech. He announced a military response in Syria, a state of emergency, a call to citizens to join the civic reserve, and a constitutional reform including the removal of French citizenship from convicted terrorists (Section 2). These policies were addressed to distinct audiences and carried a variety of messages: they were drawing the boundaries of the national community; asserting the might of the state and the determination of the Executive; creating opportunities to partake in national defence; and supposed to bolster political unity.

Lastly, doing better implies a process of learning (and being seen to have learned) between the different episodes of a crisis (Boin et al., 2010: chapter 6). The French executive learnt from the mistakes made in January: in November, it gave schools time to prepare children and their teachers for the minute of silence (Ledoux, 2022). Repetition erodes the likelihood of 'rally around the flag effects' occurring (Baum, 2002; Williams, Koch, and Smith, 2013). It leads to a weariness that political authorities must consider in their symbolic management of the situation. During the Covid-19 pandemic for instance, citizens were much more compliant to the rules (lockdown) during the first wave than during the following ones. And what is true for the people, it is also true for the Opposition.

When analysing the context in which the management of a particular crisis takes place, one also needs to consider the proximity to an election. In January 2015 for instance, no election was scheduled before several months and it was easy to lull the Opposition into unusual demonstrations of support for the incumbent. They joined the Republican March and professed political loyalty. But in November, however, regional elections were only weeks away. The Opposition was divided, and their behaviour was guided by their electoral ambitions: they talked about 'solidarity with the Government' instead of 'national unity'; and if they supported the President during the Versailles Congress, they launched scathing attacks in the National Assembly two days later. The citizenship reform was a concession to their demands that contributed to maintaining a political unity much more fragile than in January. The electoral landscape had changed by July 2016, when the city of Nice was the target of another attack. More precisely, the Right was preparing for the November primary that would select its presidential candidate: local right-wing political actors with electoral ambition abandoned the pretence of national political unity. They attacked the failure of the Executive, forcing the President to adopt a defensive tone in his speeches (Boussaguet and Faucher, 2018).

This section has shown how time and timing weigh on the strategic symbolic policy decisions that are available and how those are selected and deployed by public authorities. The comparative analysis of the French Government's responses to the terrorist attacks of 2015 and 2016 illustrates how such policies are designed based on available procedures and experiences, but also adapted to context-specific needs. Those needs include the parameters of a given situation and extend to political and strategic considerations for public actors, as incumbents of institutional positions and as individuals or members of teams. Although we have here focused on exceptional circumstances, it is clear to us that time and timing are always weighing on symbolic policies. In the next section, we turn to the agency of public authorities when they choose how to use the symbolic in the pursuit of their objectives.

7 The Symbolic, Structure, and Agency

We have seen in previous sections that the symbolic is a ubiquitous, enduring, and pervasive feature of public policy. It is taken very seriously by political actors despite being neglected by analysts. We have also argued that crises are good opportunities to observe the symbolic choices made by policymakers – we take this category as inclusive and consider that our analytic frame is potentially applicable to a diversity of contexts (national or subnational or community level) in which policies are produced. In this section, we consider how and why leaders pursuing similar objectives use quite different references and symbolic practices from a country to another. For instance, as the pandemic hit European countries in early 2020, national leaders sought to obtain the support and the compliance of their population, yet they invoked distinct collective memories of the past to convey the magnitude of the crisis and prepare their citizens for unpopular decisions. Indeed, contrasting the symbolic work performed by governments underlines the existence of national repertoires derived from the imaginaries and political institutions, as well as choices. To make sense of their symbolic policy decisions, we argue that we need to consider more than the available repertoires and also take into account leaders' agencies and character-istics. We thus discuss the influence of leaders' skills, of their institutional settings, and of the specific context on their actions and decisions.

7.1 Repertoires of Symbolic Action

Charles Tilly seminally coined the phrase 'repertoires of collective action' (Tilly, 1995; 2004) the array of practices which have been tried and tested by previous social movements and are available to newcomers as they decide what are the best means to defend their cause. He argued that, at any given time, social movement entrepreneurs choose the more appropriate actions from a bank of available options; that these options are remnants of past political conflicts and have been shaped by their institutional and political contexts; that these options are adopted and adapted as well as enriched with new stratagems and innovations. The notion of repertoire draws attention to continuities and traditions in the forms of contentious action available to political actors.

We argue that similar patterns can be identified in the realm of symbols used by public authorities. Confronted with an emergency which may present many unique features, decision-makers are rarely in uncharted territory and always try to reduce uncertainty by seeking the existence of a precedent. Thus, they turn to pre-existing protocols and procedures that have worked in prior comparable circumstances and might be expected by the population. We call 'repertoires of symbolic action' the stock of images, narratives, objects, traditions, buildings, practices, representations, songs, gestures, and historical references that are available to political authorities and from which they draw, often routinely. Some symbols or references are shared by European countries – notably because they derive from the nature of the liberal representative regime, from the intense historical connections between them, or are upheld as democratic values enshrined in the European Union. Yet, if we consider individual coun-tries, these repertoires are also quite different: even in a small region of the world such as Europe, historical events have been experienced differently and national cultures are shaped by cultural, religious, social, and political cleav-ages. The national imaginaries are thus linked to processes of state construction and narratives about it: for example, the existence of temporal ruptures through revolution or crisis; independence, secession, or merger; military occupation, defeat or victory; the adequation between national, political, or administrative boundaries; the existence of ethnic, linguistic or religious minorities; conceptions of the individual and her relationship with the community; of industrialisation; of welfare provisions. This literature is simply too vast to do it justice.

It is interesting to briefly contrast here countries that can claim a long history as a nation state, such as France and the UK, to others in which the current state is a relatively recent creation, such as Germany or Italy. For the former, the symbolic of the state involves historic palaces, gilded furniture, ceremonial guards, pomp, and ceremony surrounding monarchs and presidents. By contrast, despite its rich cultural heritage, Italy was only united in the second part of the nineteenth century. D'Azeglio, who contributed to the creation of modern Italy, wrote in his memoirs: 'unfortunately we have made Italy, but we have not created the Italians' (Cheles and Sponza, 2001: 1). Strong local-level dynamics undermine the capacity of the state and regionalism weakens national political culture because it generally entails the development of rival and antagonistic political liturgy (Ridolfi, 2012). Moreover, after WWII, political authorities worked hard to distance themselves from the legacy of fascism, which had tried to impose a 'civic religion' (Pécout, 2009; Lazar, 2014). Consequently, Italy has largely been characterised by the opposition between Christian Democrats and the socialist-communist subculture – 'two hostile nations that face each other' (Musiedlak, 1995: 60). These tensions have not been resolved by the creation of the 'Second Republic' in the 1990s and television, which became central during the Berlusconi era, durably undermined the construction of an agreed national narrative (Ridolfi, 2012: 434–435). However, since 1998, several laws have imposed the use of the national flag and of the national anthem, promoted historic monuments, introduced a Republic Day, and created civil ceremonies, thereby contributing to the construction of a new 'republican patriotism' (Ridolfi, 2012: 424–425). In a context characterised by the paucity of shared symbols, one can understand Conte invoking hugs (*abbracciarsi*) as the sign of a return to normality – a practice uniting Italians but banned by sanitary rules (Boussaguet, Faucher, and Freudlsperger, 2023). However, it was significant that President Mattarella talked about national pride and that Italians spontaneously started singing the national anthem on balconies and decorated their houses with the national flag.

To find uncontested and positive symbols of national identity is also a challenge in Germany, due to the Federal Republic's need to create a clear opposition to the past: the Prussian Empire (seen as imperialist and undemocratic), the Weimar Republic (seen as precarious and unstable), the Third Reich (for obvious reasons), and the (East) German Democratic Republic (an authoritarian regime) are all regarded as counter-examples and do not represent today a source of political identification in Germany (Greiffenhagen, M. and Greiffenhagen, S. 2002). Moreover, the over-use of symbols in earlier, failed systems also contributed to the German repertoire of symbolic actions being both ahistorical and sparse (Lübbe, 1981). The *Ersatz* symbolic culture developed to compensate for the lack of acceptable national symbols was built on democratic values such as consensus-orientation, rationality, accountability, and transparency. In this sense, there are still clear reverberations of the Protestant tradition to be found in the Federal Republic's political and symbolic culture (Berg-Schlosser and Rytlewski, 1993: 228). This sobriety is at play in the Berlin Republic's political architecture (Barnstone, 2004: 2) as well as in the staging of governmental politics during the Covid pandemic. Angela Merkel's televised address of 16 March serves as a good example: the Chancellor's desk, two flags, and the Reichstag in the background. That was all the symbolism the chancellery deemed necessary or appropriate for the occasion.

An interesting contrast is to be found in the historical references used to impress citizens with the magnitude of the pandemic crisis and the resilience of the country: Conte referred to the collapse of the Genoa bridge (in August 2018) to remind Italians of their capacity to stand together, while military metaphors and memories of WWII dominated in France and in the UK. The virus was depicted as 'the enemy' and the healthcare systems presented as 'the frontline' in the battle against it; Macron called for a 'general mobilisation', announced the deployment of a field hospital and army support for hospitals (12 March 20), and repeated six times 'we are at war' in a single speech (16 March 2022). In the UK, references to the war reflected the growing severity of the situation: Johnson initially announced that his government 'must act like any wartime government' and, a few days later, was confronted with 'the most terrible threat faced by the country since 1945'. Finally, memories of the war were prompted by Queen Elizabeth's speech delivered on 5 April, the day her Prime Minister was hospitalised. The Queen remembered her first ever radio broadcast (during the Blitz) and concluded her intervention with a comforting 'we will meet again', directly quoting a popular wartime song.

7.2 The Agency of Policymakers

If the symbolic management of a crisis is highly influenced by the existence of national, distinctive repertoires of symbolic action, it is not fully determined by them. Indeed, we need to reintroduce the agency of policymakers, who select from these available options according to their interpretation of the situation and in relation to their objectives. Moreover, it is important to note that the existence of a well-furnished national repertoire does not necessarily imply fluency or better use of the symbolic in policymaking or in crisis management. Nor does the number of symbolic references imply that the messages will be more appropriately coded and then decoded by the public. Thus, paradoxically, the most effective mobilisation of the symbolic may not be the feat of the political actors who are most convinced about the importance of the symbolic dimension of policy or the keener to connect themselves, or their actions, to a grand or national narrative. Whilst the proliferation and juxtaposition of symbols – such as in the staging of the State of the Union speech, the Queen's speech, or the rarer French President's address to the Congress in Versailles – is not detrimental to their evocative powers, it is important to ensure that they are received by the targeted audiences. Moreover, their power lies in their capacity to imply, to hint, and thus to elicit cognitive and affective reactions to their associated meanings. Rhetorically, this often means that the most efficient symbolic messages are often short, condensed, and elliptical – simple vocabulary, repetition, references that are immediately recognisable by the many. A symbol that needs to be explained by press secretaries or journalists is poorly chosen.

We illustrate this with Covid-19-related examples. In March 2020 for instance, the British Government used the mantra 'Stay home, Protect the NHS, Save lives' to carry practical and symbolic information. It invoked the National Health Service, an institution established after WWII, to evoke the solidarity and resilience of the British population. The Government called on the country to fight together (this time, against the virus) and referred to a treasured institution that not only protects individuals but needs to be protected itself. This counteracted the perception that policies pursued by Conservative governments underfunded and undermined the NHS. It was reinforced by Johnson's gratitude to the health service, made credible by his recovery from a Covid infection in an NHS hospital. The NHS thus became part and parcel of British greatness, and a symbol of resistance to the pandemic. Interestingly, Johnson also thought it important to draw attention to national solidarity, declaring 'there is such a thing as society' and directly contradicting Thatcher's famous quote ('there's no such thing as society', 1987).

On the contrary, too many references or allusive ones that are not widely understandable may cause the leaders to miss their objectives in their attempt to harness the symbolic. President Macron's rhetoric during the first wave of the Covid pandemic was at times obscure. He picked historic references that made little sense to many citizens, either because they are too dated (and could only be understood by generations who knew the title of the 1944 program of the French Resistance) or because he referred to them in such an allusive way that they could not be easily deciphered. For instance, in the same speech, he alluded to the 1789 Declaration of Rights of Man and of the Citizen by barely mentioning 'these words, the French people wrote them more than 200 years ago' and he hinted at the end of WWII with 'the concord' and 'better days'. The proliferation of symbolic references and the juxtaposition of war and of daily life (errands, readings, and dog walking) also muddled the message. Finally, Macron indulged in several long (twice the length of his European counterparts) formal TV speeches, including many references to the Nation and historical moments, and involving a careful staging with props. All this did not achieve a better communication outcome than Merkel, with her single, sober, and short televised intervention. In fact, the symbolic is interesting as a communication device because it makes possible to say little while implying much more. It relies on interpretative ambiguities: marches without signs or songs allow maximum participation of people, who would disagree if meanings were explicit. More is not always better.

7.3 Leadership Styles and Personas

Whereas the crisis-management literature generally uses 'a more task-related than person-related perspective on crisis leadership' (Boin et al., 2010: 9), we argue here that symbolic policies bear the mark of the personality and the qualities of those who choose them (Helms, 2012; Rhodes and Hart, 2016). By reference to the notion developed in the literature on public performance (Gaffney, 2014; Finlayson, 2021), we propose to take into account the '*personas*' of the leaders who choose and enact these policies.

Scholars of political leadership consider three dimensions that contribute to defining individual styles (Cerny, 1988; Drake, 2002). The first dimension relates to the rules pertaining to the institutional role of the leader, which frame and shape her actions. Indeed, 'the embedded norms and institutional characteristics (...) markedly constrain the range of responses that public leaders can consider and implement' (Boin et al., 2010: 8). The nature of the political system (presidential or parliamentary) and the unitary or federal structure of the state provide the 'constitutional staging of performances' (Finlayson, 2021: 10). The French President, who is both the head of state and the chief of the executive in a unitary and centralised state, commands resources far in excess of what the German Chancellor can yield as the head of a federal government. Indeed, whilst Macron could present himself as the ultimate 'decider' in 2020, Merkel played a different part – though not necessarily less effective or decisive – as arbiter and negotiator coordinating the policies of the *Länder*.

The second dimension refers to the broader context that surrounds the leader. It includes what the Germans call the *Zeitgeist*, the defining spirit or mood of a particular period of history, the trends and fashions, the ideas, and beliefs of the time. Information and communication technologies, the party system, and ideological cleavages also contribute to shaping the context. They guide, for instance, how the leadership will address the population. In 1953, the decision to broadcast the coronation of Elizabeth II transformed the sovereign's relation to her people, just as, over twenty years prior, President Roosevelt had used the radio to engage in 'fireside chats' with the American people (Roosevelt, 2008). In 2020, political leaders used social media (Twitter, Instagram, Facebook, etc.) alongside more traditional channels to address citizens. This has allowed them to reach different segments of the population, such as the young and urban who tend to shun both radio and television. Finally, the third dimension includes the leader's skills: her resourcefulness, her knowledge and abilities, her personality, her experiences and educational background, her personal story.

Yet, a fourth, performative dimension is still missing: indeed, political leadership is expressed in a dynamic relation between the actor and her public. To be effective, 'it is often not enough merely to possess certain qualifications, skills, or characteristics; one has to convincingly *show* them as well as *tell* people about them' (Finlayson, 2021: 475). Gofman demonstrated how the stylisation of the role is as important to a professional as her expertise and knowledge: she must impress or give a good impression of competence on top of being competent (Goffman, 1990). Leaders are expected to show leadership, to engage in an interaction with their audience, and to be convincing. In a crisis, one may note a rally-around-the flag effect, which amounts to a temporary credit given to the incumbent, but this credit will only last so long as she can maintain the impression that she is doing her job well. Her rhetorical abilities – although the talent of speechwriters surely helps – combine with personal attributes and character.

In France, the atypical political regime combines a parliamentary system with a strong presidential figure endowed with remarkable powers, particularly when he also commands a parliamentary majority. Moreover, in creating such a powerful institution in 1958, De Gaulle granted the role with ceremonial and symbolic attributes of the state. The President is constitutionally in charge of security and international affairs and is as such the 'father of the Nation'. He is the first of the French and the incarnation of the will of the people because he is directly elected (since 1962). Of course, incumbents have tried to impart their own personal style on their presidency and endeavoured to distinguish themselves from their predecessors – even if this personal style is ultimately constrained by its institutional function. Sarkozy's hyperactivity and his penchant for celebrities contributed to an incarnation of the Presidency as a super Prime Minister in charge of everyday and everybody's affairs. In reaction, Hollande decided to perform the opposite and declared he would be « normal » (Gaffney, 2015). Macron, in turn, criticised the idea of an ordinary man being at the helm and explained that his ambition was to restore the historic and majestic dimension of the presidential role. He spelt out his hierarchical interpretation of the role in press interviews. For him, 'the presidential function needs to be performed by someone who must lead the society thanks to convictions, actions and by giving a clear meaning to their approach'.[6] Indeed, his electoral victory in May 2017 was the opportunity for an impressive show in the central courtyard of the Louvre.[7] So much so that his performance has been called 'Jupiterian'.

It is therefore little surprising that Macron has seized the opportunities offered by the management of successive crises. He peppers his speeches with historical references, delivers them from the golden surroundings of the Élysée, and presents himself as the strict father protecting the French people. In March 2020, he posed as commander-in-chief in a 'war' against an 'enemy'; he called his fellow citizens to a 'sacred union' and pleaded for a 'general mobilisation'. The war lexicon was backed by his physical performance: the solemn tone, the admonition of those tempted not to abide by his rulings, the fines distributed by the police to those who did so. The rhetoric was intended to impress a sense of urgency and to characterise the magnitude of the crisis. It also served to justify the suspension of individual freedoms. By comparison, when Hollande was confronted to terrorism, he comported himself as a 'normal' – read low key – president but his symbolic performance was none the lesser: he was seen rather than heard; he spoke little and let symbols convey ambiguous but oecumenical messages (Boussaguet and Faucher, 2017: 178).

To understand Angela Merkel's leadership style, one needs to take into account the institutional context as well as the intersectional personality traits (Davidson-Schmich, 2011: 332) that contributed to shaping her *persona*. Let us consider how these features may influence how she consequently uses the symbolic. First, she was brought up in an authoritarian regime in which freedom of speech was restricted and where flamboyance and extraversion could be dangerous. Yet, in the socialist Republic, higher expectations were placed on women playing a role among the workforce and in public life than in the Federal Republic. Secondly, Merkel received a religious education (her father was a Lutheran pastor) rather than a socialist *Jugendweihe* (coming of age cere-mony) which amounted to an unusual upbringing in the generally atheist German Democratic Republic. Her socialisation influenced her relationship to power, teaching her distance, humility, and sobriety. Moreover, Merkel received

---

[6] *Challenges*, 16 October 2016. See also *Le Monde*, 04 November 2018.
[7] www.youtube.com/watch?v=2cJh_v5mmuc.

a PhD in Physics and her approach to public policy problems has often been described as non-dogmatic, informed, and rational. She herself describes this process as 'think, consult, decide' (Davidson-Schmich, 2011: 333). Whilst she showed as Chancellor an aversion to a 'too overt leadership role', she performed it with steadfastness. During the pandemic, she adopted a sober approach and a didactic tone. She presented scientific evidence to justify measures intended to curb the spread of the pandemic. She introduced corrections to ineffective policies and emphasised the complexity and fluidity of an ever-evolving situation. She endeavoured to be a non-political expert (*unpolitischer Fachmann*), a role that was facilitated by the nature of the German State.

7.4 Learning How to Deploy the Symbolic

As we have seen, symbolic policy choices are influenced by the repertoire of symbolic action, by the *personas* and individual strategies of the decision-makers, and, finally, by the contingent circumstances and the specificity of the situation. It is interesting to consider how experience, in turn, may impact policy choices and decisions relative to the use of the symbolic. Such learning effects may affect the *persona* of the leader, the evaluation of the role of the symbolic, and how to do so. One can expect that isolated incidents are more likely to lead to the reproduction of previous responses. When a situation emerges, indeed, one of the first tasks of advisors and staff is to look at precedent, to seek ready-made policies that have passed the test of time and could be adopted or adapted easily. Repetition, but also experience of previous uses of the symbolic more generally, may alter the attitude and expectations of policymakers, and of their teams.

When Hollande was elected President, he announced his intention to remain 'close to the people and able to understand them' (TV debate, 2 May 2012). To do so, he intended to shun the pomp and the ceremony of office, to be 'normal'. He soon had to renounce the idea of living in his own flat and using the Elysée as an office, but he nevertheless resisted changing many of the habits and relationships he had developed. He reluctantly accepted the protocol and the rules that govern the office of the Presidency (Gaffney, 2015). He may have been the least likely to embrace the emphatic part expected of a President, yet when Paris was hit by terrorists in January 2015, he endorsed the habit and the role, as we've seen earlier.

Yet, when a third major attack hit France (in Nice) on 14 July 2016, the symbolic responses planned by the government were deliberately low key because opinion research had warned that they were likely to be confronted with a backlash. By then, the rhetoric of national unity and solidarity or the consoling gestures of mourning could no longer uphold the world-as-if the state could protect against violence: they appeared as 'merely symbolic'. This is not so much because the rituals were any different but because the repetition of drama had changed the attitude of the audience. Rituals are often seen as contributing to the status quo and upholding the legitimacy of power holders, but they are also opportunities for challenge (Dirks, 1992). Indeed, the Prime Minister was booed at a ceremony held locally a few days later whilst the President played it safe: he walked to the Interior Ministry for a minute of silence in the company of police officers. He only travelled to the site itself three months later.

Similarly, during the Covid-19 pandemic, some political actors drew lessons from their experiences and/or learnt from abroad. Thus, some leader *personas* changed through time, which contributed to different symbolic strategies. Macron's management of the Covid crises illustrates this rather well. In March 2020, he adopted a 'Jupiterian' posture: he sought to guide and reassure by embodying the verticality of power and multiplying complex and obscure historical references. A few months later, as the second wave arrived, he abandoned the grand national narrative: he adopted a more direct and horizontal style, closer to the tone adopted by his colleagues during the first wave in Italy, Germany and in the UK. It is therefore crucial not to consider the leader's *persona* as a static variable.

We have seen in this section how policymakers draw inspiration for symbolic responses from an existing repertoire of tried and tested symbols, that their choices are guided by institutional context and the specificities of the policy-problem at hand. We have argued that these choices can be better understood if one also considers the *personas* decision-makers seek to perform. Finally, the duration of the crisis or its repetition are also constraints. What is an appropriate response to an isolated event loses its efficacy with repetition – successive attacks or waves of the pandemic (Section 6).

8 The Effects of the Symbolic

So far, we have shown how policymakers use the symbolic to convey messages to their audiences and that their efforts imply an expectation that these are poten-tially effective strategies. Yet, the precise effects of using the symbolic in public policy may be all the more difficult to measure as it is impossible to prove causal relationships between policy decisions and the evolution of public attitudes and citizens' representations and perceptions. We suggest exploring strategies to effectively make this kind of evaluation and present studies attempting to assess these effects. Our approach involves delving into counterfactuals, suggesting that one can infer impacts by contrasting anticipated and actual public reactions in response to the symbolic messages articulated by those in power. Additionally, we highlight effects uncovered through public opinion research and advocate for an approach centred on policy reception.

8.1 What Effects Are to Be Expected from Symbolic Policy?

As we have seen in Section 1, the symbolic is an interesting resource for those in power because it combines two different dimensions that may have an effect on citizens: a cognitive one and an emotional one. The first dimension is useful because it relies on condensed meanings. It thus allows the parsimonious expression of complex notions that could not be easily, or innocuously, spelt out. Moreover, such capacity to condense diverse, and sometimes contradictory, meanings implies that they can be perceived and interpreted quite independently by different social groups. The second dimension relates to the emotional resonance of symbols. Turner, amongst others, considers that they trigger reactions and drive action (Turner, 1987). They, for instance, contribute to signal the appropriate behavioural response to participants and audiences (Mariot, 2001). However, the observation of institutionalised behaviour, such as waving and cheering the President on official visits, should be analysed with caution. Although it is tempting to interpret the cheers as the expression of enthusiasm or support, Mariot warns against the illusion of inferring the emotions experienced by the crowd. As political analysts, we are better focusing on their political and social effects (Collins, 2004). Symbols serve as signposts or markers of identities, institutions, and solidarities. In some contexts, like situations of crisis, the very absence of expected symbolic action or artefact is likely to be noticed: failing to perform some of the symbolic actions that the public anticipates has been shown to be damaging for the incumbent. Not landing in New Orleans after Hurricane Katrina was for instance a major symbolic error of G.W. Bush. It was taken as an offense by victims and seen as indicative of a failure to perform the required presidential role (Boin, Brown, and Richardson, 2019). Many other leaders have come to regret not responding appropriately to crisis situations by not visiting the site or leaving to others the task of expressing empathy.

There is another dimension of symbolic public action that derives from the cognitive pole and the polysemy of symbols. When public authorities use them, they may be expecting the invocation and activation of specific repertoires of meanings in the targeted publics. As we have argued, political actors are well aware of the potential effects of using symbols. Whilst we have mostly talked about symbols that policymakers draw from existing repertoires (Section 7), others are constructed anew to be used as policy instruments. The European Union is an interesting case in point as it is a relatively recent creation and a hybrid institution that has deliberately chosen, and worked hard, to establish symbols to represent itself, such as a flag, an anthem, a motto, or Europe Day. This 'symbol' policy has been quite successful: the majority of European citizens recognise them, correctly associate them with the EU, and express some positive feelings towards Europe as an abstract idea (Foret and Trino, 2022). Interestingly, member states have been reluctant to yield to the EU the right to adopt attributes that would be too 'state-like' and going as far as removing them from the 2007 Treaty! The paradox is that, whilst they are recognised, they remain 'floating signifiers' allowing anyone to project their own vision (Foret and Trino, 2022: 4). The European Union is also a good example of the instrumentalisation of symbols for policy objectives: it has created over ninety distinct prizes (for research and innovation, economic governance, environmental, and territorial policies) that it uses to mobilise civil society in a market-driven conception of policymaking (Foret and Vargovčíková, 2021). Similar policies were developed by the New Labour governments in the UK at the end of the 1990s to govern behaviours (Faucher-King and Le Galès, 2010). However, they combined carrots and sticks (rewards and punishments) to reduce the inherent ambiguity of the tool.

The fact that symbols can be interpreted differently introduces complexity and a degree of uncertainty in policy decisions. For instance, a message read by some as reaffirming the existence and cohesion of the group may be understood by others as drawing group boundaries and therefore contributing to exclusionary moves. The failure of Hollande's constitutional reform proposal in November 2015 illustrates well the divergent reactions of political groups to new citizenship rules for dual nationals. The proposal had been tested in opinion surveys by the *Service d'Information du Gouvernement* (SIG) for several months and proven to be widely supported. It had been repeatedly demanded by the right-wing opposition. It was quickly included in the presidential speech to Congress after the November attacks in 2015 as a political concession with little impact, likely considered to be uncontroversial. However, the Élysée had overlooked that the policy clashed with the ideals of its parliamentary majority. Consequently, it triggered a cascade of emotional debates, the resignation of the Justice Minister, and much political posturing until the withdrawal of the reform. 'Symbolic' policies, in the sense of those that are anticipated to have little or no effect, may turn out to have major political consequences.

8.2 How Are Effects Studied?

We know that incumbents use the symbolic and anticipate effects that include: (1) a differential impact on social groups; (2) changes in collective representations or in the saliency of issues, social categories, and frames; (3) and changes in behaviours. But what about the evaluation of such effects? How are these assessed by public authorities and by academic research? Is the neglect of the symbolic dimension of public policy, that we identify in Section 2, linked to the absence of effects detected by research?

The effects of public policy, and particularly the effects of symbolic public policy, have featured high on elected politicians' agenda, eager to sustain their support amongst the electorate. Since the 1930s in the US for instance, the executive branch of government has paid significant and growing attention to public opinion. The White House benefits from a large opinion research budget for quantitative and qualitative surveys as well as a dedicated team of experts (Druckman and Jacobs, 2015). Information about the state of public opinion is collected and integrated in the preparation and articulation of policy to audiences. Yet, the study of these effects has largely been confined to the professionalised communication experts and policy advisers, whilst political scientists working on public opinion have paid little attention to it. One reason for such limited academic investigations lies with the perceived political sensitivity of such data collection and the subsequent discretion or evasiveness of public authorities on the question. Indeed, it is feared, in pluralist systems, that such information provides undue advantage to those who can access it. Therefore, governments are timid about acknowledging how much intelligence they have about public opinion and, even more, how they use what they have to tailor messages. This is somewhat paradoxical as democratic governments are expected to be listening to public demands, which they need to assess in order to develop responsive policies and to communicate them effectively. In France, for instance, a dedicated service (the Government Information Service or SIG) exists under the authority of the Prime Minister, responsible for the coordination of governmental communication about policies and the collection of information about public reactions to said policies. But the revelations that President Sarkozy spent a considerable budget on opinion surveys dedicated to his personal political benefit triggered a reaction and subsequent restrictions. In Germany, revelations about the uses of public opinion by the executive emerged fortuitously when a journalist required transparency (Belot and Schnatterer, 2021). And in Canada, only oral reports were provided to the executive for fear that traces could later be found about how public speech is influenced by such intelligence (Page, 2006).

Public policy studies, as a discipline, have tended to leave the analysis of policy impact on different publics to specialised subfields of social sciences. Moreover, policy evaluation has primarily focused on material, economic, quantifiable effects. However, research on policy implementation now includes a literature that considers the feedback effects of policy on policymaking processes (mediated by the ways in which the target populations are changed), analyses of the agency of 'street-level bureaucrats', and the reception of a policy by its public (Mettler and Soss, 2004; Lipsky, 2010; Revillard, 2018). We discuss below some of the research avenues that appear to be promising to seize the effects of a symbolic policy.

8.3 Is Symbolic Policy Effective?

Research on the US Presidency has benefitted from access to the extensive Presidential Archives. It sheds interesting light on the ways in which incumbents aspire to shift or shape public opinion (Jacobs and Shapiro, 2000: 194–195). Several strategies are used. Firstly, knowledge about the saliency of issues allows politicians to appear 'in tune' with public opinion (Druckman et al., 2004). Secondly, it is possible to raise the saliency of preferred issues and place them on the public agenda. The argument is that presidential rhetoric, even in the absence of policy announcements or ideological positioning, contributes to raising the attention of the public to the issue (Cohen, 1995; Canes-Wrone, 2006). Another priming effect is linked to the use of symbols of the Presidency or images of the White House (Druckman and Jacobs, 2015) in order to remind the audience of the authority or credibility associated with the orator. The influence of presidential rhetoric on the public agenda is not linked to the fact that it contains new policy announcements or express ideological positions (Cohen, 1995), content that one would consider to be substantive. On the contrary, the rise in public attention to some issues is generally due to the fact that they are mentioned, sometimes in vague and general terms in State of the Union speeches. Cohen attributes to the President's authority the lasting impact it has on public opinion, particularly in the 'reserved' domain of foreign affairs. Although he merely analyses the text (the rhetoric), it is important to note that the speeches used in his study are ritual events which are staged to underline the power positions and relations of US governmental institutions. His argument is that the importance of the issue is reinforced by the credibility of the source and its authority on the subject matter, which restrains the counter influence of alternative leaders of opinion. Thirdly, the symbolic can be used to manipulate or impose their frames (Chong and Druckman, 2007): for instance, by raising concerns about terrorism in order to render restrictions on civil liberties acceptable (Druckman and Jacobs, 2015) or by helping the executive choose more effective arguments (Heith, 2003). Situations of emergency reinforce such effects because they create a temporal bubble in which public authorities are often the main source of credible information, giving them a temporal advantage in the assertion of their interpretation of the events (Section 6). Fourthly, this can be enhanced by the language of public speeches if it is tailored with phrases and frames that resonate with their target audience. All things considered, the success of such efforts appears to be both real and limited (much weaker than authorities would hope for) (Jacobs and Shapiro, 2000: 27), but the practice remains. For instance, the French government talked much about the restauration of authority (public, parental, etc.) in 2024, as they shore up support on the right in anticipation of a far-right victory in the European parliamentary elections.

In Europe as well, public opinion research has endeavoured to capture the impact of symbolic policies on citizens' perceptions and behaviours. We have looked at the terrorist attacks in Paris and the Covid crisis as key examples in our analysis. Two studies delve into the impact of the executive's symbolic policies in these specific contexts. Firstly, Tiberj, who tracks the long-term trends of attitudes to minorities in France, notes that the attacks of January 2015 did not reverse the steady growth of tolerance (Tiberj, 2022), in contrast with shifts in public opinion after 9/11 in the US. He attributes such a difference to the frames promoted by public authorities in the aftermath of the terrorist attacks: whilst the US President insisted on the war against evil and emphasised the responsibility of Islamic terrorists, his French counterpart focused attention (Section 5) on national unity and solidarity between faith groups in a bereaved national community (Ledoux, 2022). In contrast, in 2007, his predecessor's rhetoric against migrants and Islam had been followed by a temporary decline in the indicators of tolerance (Tiberj, 2022).

Secondly, Anderson uses the fortuitous timing of one wave of a French panel studies to assess what drove French people to comply with Covid restrictions in 2020: half of the sample was interviewed before the 16 March primetime speech in which President Macron announced lockdown and declared that the country was 'at war' with the virus. He finds that the speech played an important role and was indeed followed by a sizable increase in the take up of governmental instructions. He, moreover, shows that there were differences between social groups and that 'views of presidential performance in office mattered only after his highly publicised intervention using the symbols of state power' (Anderson, 2022: 18): belief in the executor of political authority contributed to change behaviours in ways that would have not happened otherwise, as well as also serving coordination. Anderson speculates that the martial tone has radically raised the awareness of the public health issue, sharpened the perception of a crisis, and boosted citizens' sense of duty. Finally, his analysis demonstrates that the impact of the speech performance varies according to social characteristics, that partisanship plays a limited role at that stage, and that the state used different means including persuasive messages to incite compliance. Anderson's study captures uniquely and fortuitously the timely treatment of the sampled population received, allowing him to demonstrate how citizens respond differently to the messages, the constraints and the president's performance. The ambition of the paper lies however primarily in describing the effect.

Two other promising strategies must be considered if one wants to investigate the effects of symbolic policies on different publics. The first one is more impressionistic. It is quite impossible a posteriori to reconstruct the chains of causality that would enable us to show, in a convincing way, that the communication and the symbolic work done by the executive guided and modified citizens' perceptions and representations. Using counterfactuals, we can infer some effects by comparing public reactions to what was anticipated, framed, and symbolically suggested by those in power. Thus, for instance, we can interpret the absence of social tensions and of a spiral of intolerance after the terrorist attacks in the French society as one proof that the executive's framing of the events played a part in citizens' reactions and behaviours. As the President's communication advisor explained to us: 'we can see that it worked by looking at what did not happen. What did not happen was intercommunal violence, or a settling of scores' (Boussaguet and Faucher, 2022: 86).

The second strategy is suggested by Revillard, who proposes to analyse the perceptions of one policy's public in order to better understand its reception (Revillard, 2018). In the wake of the sociology of culture, she argues that an understanding of the significations attributed to a work of art, or a symbol, are insufficient to really understand what moves individuals. She advocates empirical research exploring how individuals receive, interpret, and integrate the policy that targets them, thereby contributing to the cocreation of its effective implementation by adapting their behaviours. In other words, the reception of public policy is to be understood not only as attitudes and social representations, but also as practices, behaviours, and interactions. Such an approach is thus one of the most promising avenues of research if one is to evaluate the effects of symbolic policies.

We argued in this section that it is very difficult to demonstrate a causal relationship between symbolic policy and shifts in social representations or in political behaviours. Yet, we considered several examples of studies that show how research can explore the effects of symbolic policy on audiences and therefore assess whether the messages of policymakers have been interpreted as intended and the extent to which they are changing how audiences make sense of their actions.

9 Conclusion

This Element argues that the symbolic – a wide array of objects, ideas, and practices, etc. and their associated meanings – is omnipresent in politics and, if anything, more visible or noticeable in recent years because political actors and the media now regularly refer to it when they talk about political actions. Yet, we have seen that, for a long time, the symbolic dimension of policy has been overlooked in policy analysis (Section 2) because it clashes with fundamental positivist and rationalist ontological assumptions: the symbolic deals with the intangible (both ideas and emotions are immaterial) and it is difficult to measure. Moreover, when the symbolic is considered, it is often done narrowly or implicitly, and its specificity is thus lost. We argued that such a blinkered approach prevents us from analysing a crucial dimension of political action, and one that is taken seriously by political actors.

Therefore, the symbolic needs to be brought more into the analysis of politics and policy. To make this possible, we understand the symbolic in a broad sense so as to include images, myths, rituals, and narratives, as well as figures of speech, objects, buildings, or music. We propose to focus on three main characteristics (Section 1). Firstly, symbols condense meanings. They make it possible to express ideas – including complex ones – with a simple evocation. Secondly, the symbolic combines a cognitive content on the one hand, which refers to beliefs and ideas and allows the expression of ideas that cannot be easily spelt out; and a physical or embodied register on the other hand, that stimulates emotions and entices the public to act or react. Thirdly, the symbolic is above all communication between a source and an audience sharing meanings. Indeed, to consider the symbolic dimension of policies implies that one considers policies as a dialogue between policymakers and individuals' perceptions through an imaginary – a shared repertoire of representations. We believe that bringing the symbolic back in policy analysis will allow us to take into account not only the people who are impacted by the possible material effects of the policy, but also those whose representations are affected.

We have focused most of our analysis on responses to crises because such critical junctures suspend life-as-we-know-it, endanger the social order, and question the legitimacy of those in charge. Consequently, they require a management in which the symbolic plays a more crucial role than in other contexts. Thus, we consider that the situation that comes to be defined as a crisis acts as a magnifying glass that allows us to understand the role of the symbolic in public policies. We notably saw that politics works best when it mobilises the symbols that stimulate trust or that make decision-makers and their decisions appear legitimate and acceptable (Section 3). This is particularly salient when the latter restrict the civic and political rights that are at the foundation of liberal democratic systems (such as the right to protest or freedom of movement during states of emergency). Whether through inputs (following the will of the people) or outputs (solving problems and promoting the collective well-being), legitimation always requires the use of symbols that make-believe in the trustworthiness of those in power.

Moreover, in a situation of crisis, an important task for the leadership is to respond to the emotional and practical disruptions that have been created. To do so, governments engage in symbolic acts that reassure (Section 4) or that bolster feelings of belonging to a community (Section 5). This involves the mobilisation of a series of rhetoric tools, narratives, and gestures, some of which are ritualised (minutes of silence, flags at half mast, etc.), whilst others are adapted or made up to fit with a given situation (Republican march, the singing of the national anthem on balconies, etc.).

Unlike the crisis management literature, which adopts 'a more task-related than person-related perspective on crisis leadership' (Boin et al., 2010: 10), and the 'rally around the flag literature', which too often expects a 'mechanism' such as a 'patriotic reflex' that is neither demonstrated nor explained, we showed that public authorities take a proactive role and use the symbolic to bring a social drama to a conclusion. They are the ones who organise rituals and deliver speeches to maintain, or re-create, the mental image of a united community resisting a threat. And their personal skills, as well as their institutional role and their educational background (Section 7) influence the symbolic work they develop to respond to a crisis.

This latter point enables us to address the second main contribution of this Element related to the factors that may affect the symbolic work developed in times of crisis (Figure 1) – an issue that is not discussed in the crisis management literature. Indeed, if all the leaders facing a crisis use the symbolic to respond to it (notably to legitimate themselves and their decisions, to reassure the population and to maintain unity amongst the population), what they choose to do varies. Mainly thanks to a comparative approach – longitudinal in the case of the terrorist attacks in France in 2015 and spatial for the Covid-19 crisis in Europe – three main factors have been identified to explain such differences: the importance of the timing – management of the emergency, duration and repetition of the crisis, wear phenomena, electoral cycle and the existence of forthcoming elections (Section 6); the leaders' *persona* (personality, background, institutional role), and the existence of distinct national repertoires of symbolic action, based on history, political system, and cultures (Section 7). Of course, these repertoires are analytical tools, they are not fixed once and for all. They evolve over time because political systems are weakened by internal and external conflicts and challenges, because political and electoral cycles lead to significant transformations, because narratives and stories are told about such changes and the actors involved. For instance, the Italian symbolic repertoire has been influenced since WWII by the rejection of fascism and the will to move away from its 'civic religion' (in which national symbols were preponderant). Yet, the 2022 parliamentary elections brought neo-fascists (*Fratelli d'Italia*)

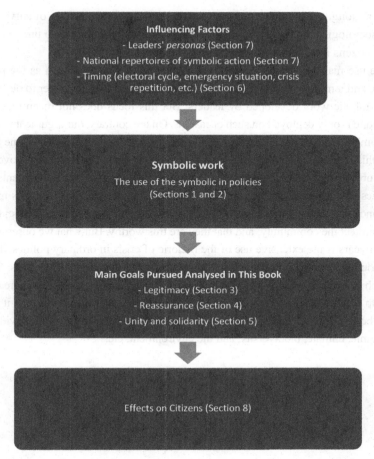

Figure 1 The use of the symbolic in response to emergency situation

back into power. Even though the very first moves of the new Prime Minister, Giorgia Meloni, privilege continuity with the previous government, one can ponder how her government will bring back the symbolic repertoire of the fascist era, and the policies it served to legitimise.

Because the symbolic conveys messages to the public who recognise them, it contributes to making policy a dialogue between policymakers and citizens, even if it is a conversation in which the former seeks to modify the representations of the latter by using its knowledge of how audiences are likely to interpret its coded messages. The successes of such attempts are difficult to measure and require research designs centred on the analysis of citizens' representations. Alternatively, one can consider (Section 8) counterfactuals (comparing public reactions to what was framed, symbolically suggested, and expected by those in power); longitudinal panel survey research (and fortuitous timing of surveys); or a sociological analysis of the reception of individual policies (to understand how citizens receive, interpret, respond and adapt to them).

We use many examples drawn from extraordinary contexts, such as the pandemic and terrorist attacks, because we believe that they make it easier to observe the symbolic work developed by leaders. But this focus does not mean that the symbolic is only deployed on such occasions. On the contrary, our argument is that the symbolic is a (more or less visible) dimension common to all policies: one just sees this more clearly when things get disrupted. Reassurance, and other governance objectives such as community building and legitimation are components of policies developed in ordinary times. For each policy, indeed, governments must convince that they are in charge; that they know what is in the public interest; that they protect the community; and that they are trustworthy. But what we observe in recent years is the extensive use of the rhetoric of crisis in ordinary politics. This rhetoric has become a useful means to manage everyday political conflicts. The French *Conseil de défense* is a good example of such symbolic work: it was created to help determine and coordinate the French policy of security and defence, it has now been deployed in many new policy sectors – health during the Covid-19 pandemic, climate, biodiversity, and the environment, etc.

References

Abélès, M. (1991). Mises En Scène et Rituels Politiques. *Hermes*, 1–2(8–9), 241–259.

Abélès, M. (1992). *La vie quotidienne au Parlement européen*. Paris: Hachette.

Anderson, B. (1991). *Imagined Communities: Reflections on the Origin and Spread of Nationalism*. London: Verso Books.

Anderson, C. J. (2022). Citizens and the State during Crisis: Public Authority, Private Behaviour and the Covid-19 Pandemic in France. *European Journal of Political Research*, 62(2), 571–593.

Andersson, J. (2018). *The Future of the World: Futurology, Futurists, and the Struggle for the Post Cold War Imagination*. New York: Oxford University Press.

Atkinson, C. L. (2019). *Semiotic Analysis and Public Policy: Connecting Theory and Practice*. New York: Routledge.

Bachrach, P., Baratz, M. S. (1963). Decisions and Nondecisions: An Analytical Framework. *The American Political Science Review*, 57(3), 632–642.

Baele, S. J., Balzacq, T. (2022). International Rituals: An Analytical Framework and Its Theoretical Repertoires. *Review of International Studies*, 48(1), 1–23.

Baker, W. D., Oneal, J. R. (2001). Patriotism or Opinion Leadership? The Nature and Origins of the 'Rally 'Round the Flag' Effect. *The Journal of Conflict Resolution*, 45(5), 661–687.

Balandier, G. (2006). *Le Pouvoir Sur Scènes*. Paris: Fayard.

Bali, V. A. (2007). Terror and Elections: Lessons from Spain. *Electoral Studies*, 26(3), 669–687.

Barker, R. (2001). *Legitimating Identities: The Self-Presentations of Rulers and Subjects*. Cambridge: Cambridge University Press.

Barnstone, D. A. (2004). *The Transparent State: Architecture and Politics in Postwar Germany*. London: Routledge. https://doi.org/10.4324/9780203799888.

Baudot, P. (2015). *Le 11-janvier: crise ou consensus?*, www.laviedesidees.fr/Le-11-janvier-crise-ou-consensus.html.

Baum, M. A. (2002). The Constituent Foundations of the Rally-Round-the-Flag Phenomenon. *International Studies Quarterly*, 46(2), 263–298.

Baum, M. A., Groeling, T. (2010). Reality Asserts Itself: Public Opinion on Iraq and the Elasticity of Reality. *International Organization*, 64(3), 443–479.

Bazin, M. (2018). Peuples en larmes, peuples en marches : La médiatisation des affects lors des attentats de janvier 2015. *Mots. Les Langages du Politique*, 118(3), 75–94.

Becker, H. S. (1997). *Outsiders*. New ed. New York: S & S International.

Bell, C. (1997). *Ritual: Perspectives and Dimensions*. Oxford University Press.

Belot, C., Schnatterer, T. (2021). Sondeurs, Sondages et Enquêtes d'opinion dans la Décision Publique. In Jacob, S., Schiffino, N., eds., *Politiques Publiques : Fondements et Prospectives Pour l'analyse de l'action Publique*. Bruxelles: Bruylant. 385–432.

Bender, J., Wellbery, D. (1991). *Chronotypes: The Construction of Time*. 1st ed. Stanford, CA: Stanford University Press.

Benford, R. D., Snow D. A. (2000). Framing Processes and Social Movements: An Overview and Assessment. *Annual Review of Sociology*, 26(1), 611–639.

Berg-Schlosser, D., Rytlewski, R. (1993). *Political Culture in Germany*. New York: Palgrave Macmillan.

Bess, M. (2003). *The Light-Green Society: Ecology and Technological Modernity in France, 1960–2000*. Chicago, IL: University of Chicago Press.

Bevir, M., Rhodes, R. A. W. (2003). *Interpreting British Governance*. London: Routledge.

Bevir, M., Rhodes, R. A. W. (2010). *The State as Cultural Practice*. Oxford: Oxford University Press.

Boin, A., Brown, C., Richardson, J. A. (2019). *Managing Hurricane Katrina: Lessons from a Megacrisis*. Baton Rouge, LA: LSU Press.

Boin, A., 't Hart, P., McConnell, A. (2009). Crisis Exploitation: Political and Policy Impacts of Framing Contests. *Journal of European Public Policy*, 16(1), 81–106.

Boin, A., 't Hart, P., Stern, P. C., Sundelius, B. (2010). *The Politics of Crisis Management: Public Leadership under Pressure*. Cambridge: Cambridge University Press.

Boussaguet, L. (2016). Participatory Mechanisms as Symbolic Policy Instruments?. *Comparative European Politics*, 14(1), 107–124.

Boussaguet, L., Faucher, F. (2017). Quand l'État convoque la rue: La Marche républicaine du 11 janvier 2015. *Gouvernement et action publique*, 6(2), 37–61.

Boussaguet, L., Faucher, F. (2018). La construction des discours présidentiels post-attentats à l'épreuve du temps. *Mots : Les Langages du Politique*, 118, 95–115.

Boussaguet, L., Faucher, F. (2020). Beyond a 'Gesture': The Treatment of the Symbolic in Public Policy Analysis. *French Politics*, 18(1–2), 189–205.

Boussaguet, L., Faucher, F. (2022). At the Upper Echelons of the State: Symbols to Build National Unity. In Faucher, F., Truc, G., eds., *Facing Terrorism in France Lessons from the 2015 Paris Attacks*. Basingstoke: Palgrave, pp. 81–92.

Boussaguet, L., Faucher, F., Freudlsperger, C. (2023). Performing Crisis Management: National Repertoires of Symbolic Action and Their Usage during the Covid-19 Pandemic in Europe. *Political Studies*, 71(4), 1090–1109.

Brody, R. (1991). *Assessing the President: The Media, Elite Opinion and Public Support*. Stanford, CA: Stanford University Press.

Canes-Wrone, B. (2006). *Who Leads Whom? Presidents, Policy, and the Public*. Chicago, IL: University of Chicago Press.

Cerny, P. G. (1988). The Process of Personal Leadership: The Case of De Gaulle. *International Political Science Review*, 9(2), 131–142.

Cheles, L., Sponza, L. (2001). *The Art of Persuasion: Political Communication in Italy from 1945 to the 1900s*. Manchester: Manchester University Press.

Chong, D., Druckman, J. N. (2007). A Theory of Framing and Opinion Formation in Competitive Elite Environments. *Journal of Communication*, 57, 99–118.

Chowanietz, C. (2016). *Bombs, Bullets, and Politicians: France's Response to Terrorism*. Montreal: McGill Queen's University Press.

Cohen, A. (1974). *Two-Dimensional Man; an Essay on the Anthropology of Power and Symbolism in Complex Society*. Berkeley, CA: University of California Press.

Cohen, J. E. (1995). Presidential Rhetoric and the Public Agenda. *American Journal of Political Science*, 39(1), 87–107.

Coleman, S. (2013). *How Voters Feel*. Cambridge: Cambridge University Press.

Collins, R. (2004). Rituals of Solidarity and Security in the Wake of Terrorist Attack. *Sociological Theory*, 22(1), 53–87.

Crewe, E. (2005). *Lords of Parliament: Manners, Rituals and Politics*. Manchester: Manchester University Press.

Davidson-Schmich, L. K. (2011). Gender, Intersectionality, and the Executive Branch: The Case of Angela Merkel. *German Politics*, 20(3), 325–341.

De Luca, M. (2020). *The Italian Style: Giuseppe Conte's 'half-Populist' Leadership during COVID-19*. LSE Blogs. https://blogs.lse.ac.uk/euro ppblog/2020/06/08/the-italian-style-giuseppe-contes-half-populist-leader ship-during-covid-19/.

Debord, G. (1967). *La société du spectacle*. Paris: les éditions Buchet-Chastel.

Deflem, M. (1991). Ritual, Anti-Structure and Religion: A Discussion of Victor Turner's Processual Symbolic Analysis. *Journal for the Scientific Study of Religion*, 30(1), 1–25.

Diehl, P. (2015). *Das Symbolische, das Imaginäre und die Demokratie. Eine Theorie politischer Repräsentation*. Baden-Baden: Nomos.

Diehl, P., Hayat S., Sintomer, Y. (2014). La Représentation Politique. *Trivium. Revue franco-allemande de sciences humaines et sociales – Deutsch-französische Zeitschrift für Geistes- und Sozialwissenschaften*, 16. https://doi.org/10.4000/Trivium.4771 .

Dirks, N. B. (1992). Ritual and Resistance: Subversion as a Social Fact. In Haynes, D. E., Prakash, G., eds., *Contesting Power: Resistance and Everyday Social Relations in South Asia*. Oakland, CA: University of California Press, pp. 213–238.

Disch, L, Mvan de Sande, M., Urbinati, N. (2020). *The Constructivist Turn in Political Representation*. Edinburgh: Edinburgh University Press.

Douglas, M. (1986). *How Institutions Think*. Syracuse, NY: Syracuse University Press.

Douglas, M. (2002). *Purity and Danger: An Analysis of Concepts of Pollution and Taboo*. London: Routledge.

Drake, H. (2002). Jacques Delors et la Commission Européenne: Un leadership unique?. *Politique Européenne*, 8, 131–145.

Druckman, J. N., Holmes, J. W. (2004). Does Presidential Rhetoric Matter? Priming and Presidential Approval. *Presidential Studies Quarterly*, 34(4), 755–778.

Druckman, J. N., Jacobs, L. R. (2015). *Who Governs?: Presidents, Public Opinion, and Manipulation*. Chicago, IL: University of Chicago Press.

Dupuy, C., Van Ingelgom, V. (2019). Policy Feedback. In Boussaguet, L., Jacquot, S., eds., *Dictionnaire Des Politiques Publiques*. Paris: Presses de Sciences Po, pp. 453–461.

Durand, G. (2003). *L'Imagination symbolique*. Paris: Presses Universitaires de France.

Durkheim, E. (1990). *Les Formes Élémentaires de La Vie Religieuse*. Paris: Presses Universitaires de France.

Dye, T. (1987). *Understanding Public Policy*. New York: Prentice-Hall.

Easton, D. (1975). A Re-Assessment of the Concept of Political Support. *British Journal of Political Science*, 5(4), 435–457.

Edelman, M. (1977). *Political Language: Words That Succeed and Policies That Fail*. New York: Academic Press.

Edelman, M. (1988). *Constructing the Political Spectacle*, 1st ed., Chicago, IL: University of Chicago Press.

Edelman, M. (2013). *Politics as Symbolic Action: Mass Arousal and Quiescence*. Cambridge: Academic Press.

Faucher-King, F. (2005). *Changing Parties: An Anthropology of British Political Party Conferences*. Basingstoke: Palgrave Macmillan.

Faucher-King, F., Le Galès, P. (2010). *The New Labour Experiment: Change and Reform under Blair and Brown*. Redwood City, CA: Stanford University Press.

Faucher, F., Boussaguet, L. (2017). The Politics of Symbols: Reflections on the French Government's Framing of the 2015 Terrorist Attacks. *Parliamentary Affairs*, 71(1), 169–195.

Faucher, F., Hay, C. (2015). Les rituels de vote en France et au Royaume-Uni. *Revue Française de Science Politique*, 65(2), 213–236.

Faucher, F. (2025). Politics as Ritual. In Hay, C. ed., *What Is Politics?* Cambridge: Polity Press.

Finlayson, A. (2021). Performing Political Ideologies. In Rai, S., Gluhovic, M., Jestrovic, S., Saward, M., eds., *The Oxford Handbook of Politics and Performance*. Oxford: Oxford University Press, pp. 471–483.

Foret, F., Trino, N. (2022). Standing for Europe: Citizens' Perceptions of European Symbols as Evidence of a 'Banal Europeanism'? *Nations and Nationalism*, 28(3), 954–971.

Foret, F., Vargovčíková, J. (2021). The Prize of Governance: How the European Union Uses Symbolic Distinctions to Mobilize Society and Foster Competitiveness. *JCMS: Journal of Common Market Studies*, 59(5), 1033–1050.

Gaffney, J. (2015). *France in the Hollande Presidency: The Unhappy Republic*. Basingstoke: Palgrave MacMillan.

Gaffney, J. (2014). Performative Political Leadership. In Rhodes R. A. W., 't Hart P., eds., *The Oxford Handbook of Political Leadership*. Oxford: Oxford University Press, pp. 389–402.

Godelier, M. (2015). *L'Imaginé, l'imaginaire & le symbolique*. Paris: CNRS.

Goffman, E. (1990). *The Presentation of Self in Everyday Life*. London: Penguin.

Göhler, G. (2013). La Dimension Affective de La Démocratie. Réflexions Sur La Relation de La délibération et de La Symbolicité. *Raisons Politiques*, 50, 97–114.

Goodin, R. E. (1980). *Manipulatory Politics*. New Haven, CT: Yale University Press.

Greiffenhagen, M., Greiffenhagen, S. (2002). *Handwörterbuch zur politischen Kultur der Bundesrepublik Deutschland*. Opladen: Westdeutscher Verlag.

Hacking, I. (2000). *The Social Construction of What?*. Revised ed. Cambridge, MA: Harvard University Press.

Hall, P. (1993). Policy Paradigms, Social Learning and the State: The Case of Economic Policymaking in Britain. *Comparative Politics*, 25(3), 275–298.

t'Hart, P. (1993). Symbols, Rituals and Power: The Lost Dimensions of Crisis Management. *Journal of Contingencies and Crisis Management*, 1(1), 36–50.

Hay, C. (2009). King Canute and the Problem of Structure and Agency: On Times, Tides and Heresthetics. *Political Studies*, 57(2), 260–279.

Hay, C. (2007). *Why We Hate Politics*. Cambridge: Polity Press.

Hay, C. (1996). Narrating Crisis: The Discursive Construction of the 'Winter of Discontent'. *Sociology*, 30(2), 253–277.

Heith, D. J. (2003). One for All: Using Focus Groups and Opinion Polls in the George H. W. Bush White House. *Congress & the Presidency*, 30(1), 81–94.

Helms, L. (2012). *Poor Leadership and Bad Governance: Reassessing Presidents and Prime Ministers in North America, Europe and Japan*. Northampton, MA: Edward Elgar.

Hetherington, M. J., Nelson, M. (2003). Anatomy of a Rally Effect: George W. Bush and the War on Terrorism. *PS: Political Science & Politics*, 36(1), 37–42.

Hunter, A. (1974). *Symbolic Communities*. Chicago, IL: University Of Chicago Press

Jacobs, L. R., Shapiro, R. Y. (2000). *Politicians Don't Pander: Political Manipulation and the Loss of Democratic Responsiveness*. Chicago, IL: University of Chicago Press.

Jarvis, L. (2022). Constructing the Coronavirus Crisis: Narratives of Time in British Political Discourse on COVID-19. *British Politics*, 17(1), 24–43.

Jones, C. O. (1970). *An Introduction to the Study of Public Policy*. Belmont, CA: Duxbury Press.

Kantorowicz, E. (2016). *The King's Two Bodies*. Princeton, NJ: Princeton University Press.

Katz, D., Dayan, E. (1994A). *Media Events: Live Broadcasting of History*. New ed. Cambridge, MA: Harvard University Press.

Kertzer, D. I. (1989). *Ritual, Politics and Power*. New ed. New Haven, CT: Yale University Press.

Kertzer, D. I. (1996). *Politics and Symbols: Italian Communist Party and the Fall of Communism*. New Haven, CT: Yale University Press.

Lakoff, G. 2002. *Moral Politics: How Liberals and Conservatives Think*. 2nd ed. Chicago, IL: University of Chicago Press.

Lasswell, H. D. (2011). *Politics: Who Gets What, When, How*. Whitefish, MT: Literary Licensing LLC.

Lazar, M. (2014). La République: une Italie plus unie ou plus désunie?. In Blanc-Chaléard, M., ed., *D'Italie et d'ailleurs*. Rennes: Presses Universitaires de Rennes, pp. 67–77.

Leach, E. (1976). *Culture and Communication*. Cambridge: Cambridge University Press.

Ledoux, S. (2022). In the Schools: Bringing Pupils into the National Community of Mourning. In Faucher, F., Truc, G., eds., *Facing Terrorism in France: Lessons from the 2015 Paris Attacks*. Basingstoke: Palgrave, pp. 55–67.

Lerner, D., Lasswell, H. D. (1951). *The Policy Sciences*. Stanford, CA: Stanford University Press.

Lipsky, M. (2010). *Street-Level Bureaucracy: Dilemnas of the Individual in Public Services*. New-York: Russell Sage Foundation.

Lübbe, H. (1981). Staat Ohne Symbole. *Die Politische Meinung*, 194, 6–10.

Lukes, S. (1975). Political Ritual and Social Integration. *Sociology*, 9(2), 289–308.

Luckmann, T., Berger, P. L. (1991). *The Social Construction of Reality: A Treatise in the Sociology of Knowledge*. New ed. London: Penguin.

Malone, E., Hultman, N. E., Anderson, K. L., Romeiro, V. (2017). Stories about Ourselves: How National Narratives Influence the Diffusion of Large-Scale Energy Technologies. www.sciencedirect.com/science/article/pii/S2214629617301640.

Mansbridge, J., Hayat, S., Talpin, J., et al. (2022). *Dispositifs de la démocratie: Entre participation, délibération et représentation*. Paris: Classiq Garnier.

Mariot, N. (2007). *C'est en marchant qu'on devient président : La République et ses chefs de l'Etat 1848–2007*. Montreuil: Aux Lieux d'être.

Mariot, N. (2001). Les formes élémentaires de l'effervescence collective, ou l'état d'esprit prêté aux foules. *Revue française de science politique*, 51(5), 707–738.

Mavelli, L. (2013). Between Normalisation and Exception: The Securitisation of Islam and the Construction of the Secular Subject. *Millennium*, 41(2), 159–181.

Mazur, A. G. (1995). *Gender Bias and the State: Symbolic Reform at Work in Fifth Republic France*. Pittsburgh, PA: University of Pittsburgh Press.

Mettler, S. (2005). *Soldiers to Citizens: The G.I. Bill and the Making of the Greatest Generation*. New York: Oxford University Press.

Mettler, S., Soss, J. (2004). The Consequences of Public Policy for Democratic Citizenship: Bridging Policy Studies and Mass Politics. *Perspectives on Politics*, 2(01), 55–73.

Michels, A. (2011). Innovations in Democratic Governance: How Does Citizen Participation Contribute to a Better Democracy?. *International Review of Administrative Science*, 77(2), 275–293.

Mueller, J. E. (1985). *War, Presidents and Public Opinion*. Lanham, MD: University Press of America.

Muller, P. (2018). *Les Politiques Publiques*. Paris: Presses Universitaires de France.

Musiedlak, D. (1995). Construction politique et identité nationale en Italie: De l'unité au fascisme. In Diamanti, I., ed., *L'Italie, une nation en suspens*. Bruxelles: Complexe, pp. 19–61.

Natale, P. (2004). Il ruolo di Berlusconi nell'evoluzione dei sondaggi in Italia. *Comunicazione Politica*, 5(1), 135–142.

Orr, G. (2015). *Ritual and Rhythm in Electoral Systems: A Comparative Legal Account*. London: Routledge.

Ozouf, M. (2015). *De Révolution en République: Les chemins de la France*. Paris: Gallimard.

Page, C. (2006). *The Roles of Public Opinion Research in Canadian Government*. Toronto, CA: University of Toronto Press.

Parsons, W. (1995). *Public Policy: An Introduction to the Theory and Practice of Policy Analysis*. Northampton, MA: Edward Elgar.

Pécout, G. (2009). Retrouver la nation des Italiens? Le sentiment national dans les régimes d'identité de l'Italie contemporaine. In Lazar, M., ed., *L'Italie contemporaine de 1945 à nos jours*. Paris: Fayard, pp. 129–141.

Permoser, J. M. (2012). Civic Integration as Symbolic Politics: Insights from Austria. *European Journal of Migration and Law*, 14(2), 173–198.

Pierson, P. (1993). Review: When Effect Becomes Cause: Policy Feedback and Political Change. *World Politics*, 45(4), 595–628.

Power, M. (1999). *The Audit Society: Rituals of Verification*. New ed. Oxford: Oxford University Press.

Radaelli, C. (2019). Récits. In Boussaguet, L., Jacquot, S., Ravinet, P., eds., *Dictionnaire Des Politiques Publiques*. Paris: Presses de Sciences Po, pp. 528–533.

Rai, S. M. (2010). Analysing Ceremony and Ritual in Parliament. *The Journal of Legislative Studies*, 16(3), 284–297.

Rai, S. M. (2015). Political Performance: A Framework for Analysing Democratic Politics. *Political Studies*, 63(5), 1179–1197.

Rai, S. M., Milija Gluhovic, Silvija Jestrovic, et Michael Saward. 2021. *The Oxford Handbook of Politics and Performance*. Oxford: Oxford University Press.

Rauer, V. (2006). Symbols in Action: Willy Brandt's Kneefall at the Warsaw Memorial. In Alexander, J. C., ed., *Social Performance*. Cambridge: Cambridge University Press, pp. 257–282.

Rein, M. (1976). *Social Science and Public Policy*. London: Penguin Books.

Revillard, A. (2018). Saisir Les Conséquences d'une Politique à Partir de Ses Ressortissants. La Réception de l'action Publique. *Revue Française de Science Politique*, 68(3), 469–491.

RFSP. (2000). Numéro Spécial: Les Approaches Cognitives Des Politiques Publiques. *Revue Française de Science Politique*, 50(2), 187–350.

Rhodes, R. A. W., Hart, P. T. (2016). *The Oxford Handbook of Political Leadership*. Reprint ed. Oxford: Oxford University Press.

Ridolfi, M. (2012). Feste civili e giorni della memoria: L'Italia della Seconda Repubblica 1994–2011. In Biaoni, M., Conti, F., Ridolfi, M., eds., *Celebrare la nazione: Grandi anniversari e memorie pubbliche nella società contemporanea*. Milan: Silvana Editoriale, pp. 417–436.

Roe, E. M. (1994). *Narrative Policy Analysis*. Durham, NC: Duke University Press.

Roosevelt, F. D. (2008). *Fireside Chats of Franklin Delano Roosevelt: Radio Addresses to the American People about the Depression, the New Deal, and the Second World War 1933–1944*. St. Petersburg, FL: Red and Black.

Rosa. H. (2020). *The Uncontrollability of the World*. Cambridge: Polity.

Saward, M. (2010). *The Representative Claim*. Oxford: Oxford University Press.

Scacco, J. (2011). A Weekend Routine: The Functions of the Weekly Presidential Address from Clinton to Obama. *Electronic Media & Politics*, 1(4), 66–88.

Scharpf, F. W. (1999). *Governing in Europe: Effective and Democratic?* Oxford: Oxford University Press.

Schattschneider, E. E. (1935). *Politics, Pressures and the Tariff, a Study of Free Private Enterprise in Pressure Politics, as Shown in the 1929–1930 Revision of the Tariff*. New York: Prentice-Hall.

Sczepanski, R. (2023). European by Action: How Voting Reshapes Nested Identities. *European Union Politics*, 24(4), 751–770.

Seligman, A. B., Weller, R. P., Puett, M. J., Simon, B. (2008). *Ritual and Its Consequences: An Essay on the Limits of Sincerity*. New York: Oxford University Press.

Simko, C. (2015). *The Politics of Consolation: Memory and the Meaning of September 11*. Oxford: Oxford University Press.

Stoker, G., Hay, C., Barr, M. (2016). Fast Thinking: Implications for Democratic Politics. *European Journal of Political Research*, 55(1), 3–21.

Stone, D. A. (1989). Causal Stories and the Formation of Policy Agendas. *Political Science Quarterly*, 104(2), 281–300.

Strathern, M. (2000). *Audit Cultures: Anthropological Studies in Accountability, Ethics and the Academy*. Abingdon: Routledge.

Suárez, S. L. (2014). Symbolic Politics and the Regulation of Executive Compensation: A Comparison of the Great Depression and the Great Recession. *Politics and Society*, 42(1), 73–105.

Surel, Y. (2019). Approches Cognitives. In Boussaguet, L., Jacquot, S., Ravinet, P., eds., *Dictionnaire Des Politiques Publiques*. Paris: Presses de Sciences Po, pp. 90–98.

Swidler, A. (1986). Culture in Action: Symbols and Strategies. *American Sociological Review*, 51(2), 273–286.

Tiberj, V. (2022). In People's Minds: An Authoritarian Dynamic or the Spread of Tolerance?. In Faucher, F., Truc, G., eds., *Facing Terrorism in France: Lessons from the 2015 Paris Attacks*. Basingstoke: Palgrave, pp. 93–105.

Tilly, C. (1995). Contentious Repertoires in Great Britain, 1758–1834. In Traugott, M. W., ed., *Repertoires and Cycles of Collective Action*. Durham, NC: Duke University Press, pp. 15–42.

Tilly, C. (2004). *Social Movements, 1768–2004*. Boulder: Routledge.

Todd, E., Laforgue, P. (2015). *Qui est Charlie? Sociologie d'une Crise Religieuse*. Paris: Seuil.

Turner, V. (1987). *Betwixt & between: Patterns of Masculine and Feminine Initiation*. Carus Mahdi, L., Foster, S., Little, M., eds. Chicago: Open Court.

Turner, V. (1970). *Forest of Symbols: Aspects of Ndembu Ritual*. Chicago: Ithaca, NY: Cornell University Press.

Turner, V. (1969). *Ndembu Divination, Its Symbolism & Techniques*. Published on behalf of the Rhodes-Livingstone Institute by the Manchester University Press.

Turner, V. (1995). *The Ritual Process: Structure and Anti-Structure*, New ed. Piscataway, NJ: AldineTransaction.

Walzer, M. (1967). On the Role of Symbolism in Political Thought. *Political Science Quarterly*, 82(2), 191–204.

Weaver, K. (1986). The Politics of Blame Avoidance. *Journal of Public Policy*, 6(4), 371–398.

Williams, L. K., Koch, M. T., Smith, J. M. (2013). The Political Consequences of Terrorism: Terror Events, Casualties, and Government Duration. *International Studies Perspectives*, 14(3), 343–361.

Wodak, R. (2009). *The Discourse of Politics in Action*. London: Palgrave Macmillan UK.

Wodak, R. (2021). Crisis Communication and Crisis Management during COVID-19. *Global Discourse*, 11(3), 329–353.

Wong, S. S. (2021). One-Upmanship and Putdowns: The Aggressive Use of Interaction Rituals in Face-to-Face Diplomacy. *International Theory*, 13(2), 341–371.

Yanow, D. (1996). *How Does a Policy Mean? Interpreting Policy and Organizational Actions*. Washington, DC: Georgetown University Press.

Yanow, D. (2000). *Conducting Interpretive Policy Analysis*. Sage University Papers Series on Qualitative Research Methods, Vol. 47. Thousand Oaks, CA: Sage.

Cambridge Elements $\equiv$

Public Policy

M. Ramesh
National University of Singapore (NUS)

M Ramesh is UNESCO Chair on Social Policy Design at the Lee Kuan Yew School of Public Policy, NUS. His research focuses on governance and social policy in East and Southeast Asia, in addition to public policy institutions and processes. He has published extensively in reputed international journals. He is co-editor of *Policy and Society* and *Policy Design and Practice*.

Michael Howlett
Simon Fraser University, British Columbia

Michael Howlett is Burnaby Mountain Professor and Canada Research Chair (Tier1) in the Department of Political Science, Simon Fraser University. He specialises in public policy analysis, and resource and environmental policy. He is currently editor-in-chief of *Policy Sciences* and co-editor of the *Journal of Comparative Policy Analysis, Policy and Society* and *Policy Design and Practice*.

Xun WU
Hong Kong University of Science and Technology (Guangzhou)

Xun WU is currently a Professor at the Innovation, Policy and Entrepreneurship Thrust at the Society Hub of Hong Kong University of Science and Technology (Guangzhou). He is a policy scientist with a strong interest in the linkage between policy analysis and public management. Trained in engineering, economics, public administration, and policy analysis, his research seeks to make contribution to the design of effective public policies in dealing emerging policy challenges across Asian countries.

Judith Clifton
University of Cantabria

Judith Clifton is Professor of Economics at the University of Cantabria, Spain, and Editor-in-Chief of *Journal of Economic Policy Reform*. Her research interests include the determinants and consequences of public policy across a wide range of public services, from infrastructure to health, particularly in Europe and Latin America, as well as public banks, especially, the European Investment Bank. Most recently, she is principal investigator on the Horizon Europe Project GREENPATHS (www.greenpaths.info) on the just green transition.

Eduardo Araral
National University of Singapore (NUS)

Eduardo Araral specializes in the study of the causes and consequences of institutions for collective action and the governance of the commons. He is widely published in various journals and books and has presented in more than ninety conferences. Ed was a 2021–22 Fellow at the Center for Advanced Study of Behavioral Sciences, Stanford University. He has received more than US$6.6 million in external research grants as the lead or co-PI for public agencies and corporations. He currently serves as a Special Issue Editor (collective action, commons, institutions, governance) for World Development and is a member of the editorial boards of *Water Economics and Policy, World Development Sustainability, Water Alternatives* and the *International Journal of the Commons*.

About the Series

Elements in Public Policy is a concise and authoritative collection of assessments of the state of the art and future research directions in public policy research, as well as substantive new research on key topics. Edited by leading scholars in the field, the series is an ideal medium for reflecting on and advancing the understanding of critical issues in the public sphere. Collectively, the series provides a forum for broad and diverse coverage of all major topics in the field while integrating different disciplinary and methodological approaches.

Cambridge Elements ≡

Public Policy

Elements in the Series

Printed in the United States
by Baker & Taylor Publisher Services